Teaching Manual
For Manners and Customs of the People of Mthwakazi

ZACCHAEUS DUBE

Copyright © 2024 by Zacchaeus Dube

All rights reserved. This book or any of its portion may not be reproduced or transmitted in any means, electronic or mechanical, including recording, photocopying, or by any information storage and retrieval system, without the prior written permission of the copyright holder except in the case of brief quotations embodied in critical reviews and other noncommercial uses permitted by copyright law.

Printed in the United States of America
Library of Congress Control Number: 2024921689
ISBN: Softcover   979-8-89518-400-4
          e-Book   979-8-89518-401-1
Published by: WP Lighthouse
Publication Date: 10/22/2024

To buy a copy of this book, please contact:
WP Lighthouse
Phone: +1-888-668-2459
support@wplighthouse.com
wplighthouse.com

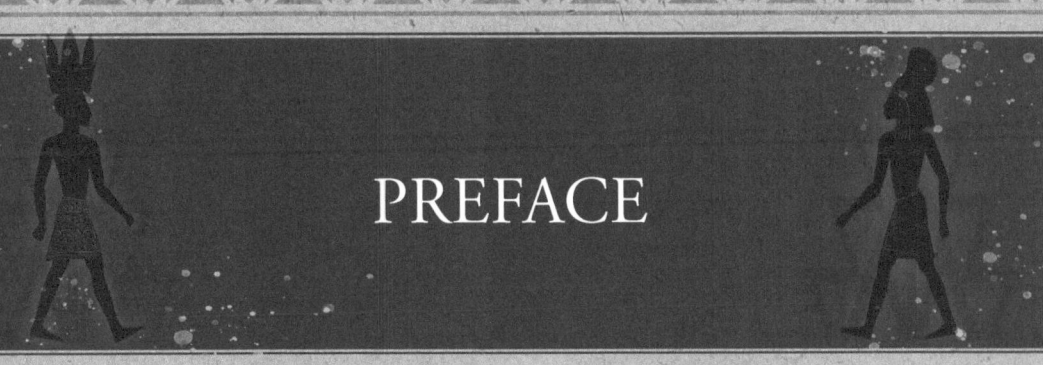

PREFACE

For my wife sithabile ndlovu dube
and our children Zakheleni, Vusumuzi, Mondleni,
gcinakele that they may uphold this legacy for
Mihwakazi religion.

In memory of
Gideon Mthembo dube (iqadi)
Sharai Moyo (ilozwi)
Matibini Makhonjwa ndlovu (isuthu)
Sethukani Moyo (ilozwi)

Compiled by
Zacchaeus Mthembo dubc, Phd, ch edu

TABLE OF CONTENTS

Introduction vii

Chapter One
Beliefs and the Concept of God 1

Chapter Two
Mthwakazi Customs and Beliefs (Imikhubo) 7

Chapter Three
Omens (Imhlolo) 11

Chapter Four
General Taboos (Amazilo) 15

Chapter Five
Taboos, Customs, and Omens Affecting Men 21

Chapter Six
Taboos, Customs, and Omens Affecting Women .. 25

Chapter Seven
Marriage and Childbearing 31

Chapter Eight
Relationship and Homemaking............................. 45

Chapter Nine
Death and Burial.. 51

Chapter Ten
**Religious Coexistence Between
the Dead and the Living** 61

Chapter Eleven
Summary 67

Footnotes 71

Bibliography 73

INTRODUCTION

In this thesis, I intend to reveal and teach the religion of Mthwakazi, a people or nation that was founded by King Mzilikazi after he moved northward, away from Zululand, the land that was ruled by Tshaka the Zulu. Mzilikazi was one of Tshaka's army generals and had been threatened by Tshaka because he had kept the loot of cattle that he had taken after a raid on the tribe of the bamangwato. Tshaka, the king of the Zulus, needed all the loot to be surrendered over to him, but Mzilikazi, with the loot, refused, and after a number of demands and threats, Mzilikazi decided to move north to seek for a free land, away from Tshaka. In the sixteenth century, two other generals had also left Zululand for free land to the north of the limpopo river. soshongana and Zwangendaba had moved before Mzilikazi. The four—Tshaka, Zwangendaba, soshongana, and Mzilikazi—were united under a culture, a language, and a religion.

This account attempts to present this magico-religion, the concepts and practices of the Mthwakazi people now occupying the southwest portion of present-day Zimbabwe, formerly rhodesia, a british colony until april 18, 1980, when it gained its independence. The religion of this nation is based upon the pre-historic baVenda religion as revealed and studied by hugh stayt in the 1920s. It focuses upon a belief in a supreme god mysteriously presiding over his creation. it is this supreme

god the people of Mthwakazi take as a fundamental concept to believe that every object animate or inanimate possesses a kinetic power for good or for evil. The social organization is complex, where each individual is a member of a number of independent groupings. i will mention four that are regarded as the most important for the teaching and learning of this religion and its culture. One belongs to a family circle, a larger group on the partrilineal lineage through which descent, succession, and inheritance are reckoned. There is a close matrilineal lineage, and we believe more angry spirits, which cause hardships, come from the mother's side. The individual also belongs to a lineage group of totemic character; the majority of which are called by some animal or creature's names.

The attitude of the people of Mthwakazi toward the sacred is displayed in beliefs and practices that run the whole gamut of religious ideas, from faith in such things like mana, animism, to belief in ancestral worship, belief in a supreme god. We call this god *uNkulunkulu*, the greatest one, also called *uMdali*, the creator. The magico-religious practices of the people of Mthwakazi are guided and taught by specialists, the shaman *inyanga* and a diviner *isangoma*. These specialists are very important people in the community as the shaman has power to cure diseases. His rigorous training in his craft qualifies him to be a specialist in a particular illness or to be a general practitioner treating all types of diseases. Using drugs from plants, emetics, and animal poison, the shaman can treat most diseases found in the community, such as malaria, rheumatism, pneumonia, insanity, and toothache, even sterility. The specialists are possessed by the spirits of the invisible to be able to dream or foretell the future. They are able to read and cast lots to determine the treatment of an illness. They help the rulers by warnings if the nation is hurting the ancestral spirits, which may cause the spirits to turn against the nation and cause disasters. Against the shamans and the diviners, the nation of Mthwakazi is afraid of two adversaries, spiritual malcontents that cause misfortunes in the nation. These are wizards and witches. These deal with bad spirits and obtain death-dealing powers, even from the shamans, to kill their enemies. Witches are believed to be women who have the spirit that can enable them to travel at night, riding brooms or hyenas and bears. They do this naked and bewitch their enemies; we believe they eat human flesh. When they die, they leave this craft with their beloved daughters. They get magic for their arts from snake poisons, plants, and animals.

Mthwakazi nation also believes in the cult of the dead. The dead play a great or primary role in their religion and religious life in general. To Mthwakazi, human souls are a combination of breath and shadow, the two elements that depart from every living creature at death. Mthwakazi people believe that the soul, after leaving the body at death, finds a new place in which to rest. We believe it may linger for a while at the grave and may reveal itself to its descendants in dreams or just glow at night, thus make its needs known to the living. Cases of reincarnation, especially of chiefs or kings, are believed in when a lion or leopard, even a snake, may be seen and considered a reincarnation of the dead king. These animals are seen many times with unusual features; some with only three legs, some with only one ear. This will be indicative of the nature of message therein. When anybody dies, every relative tries to be present at the deathbed because being absent is associated with suspicion of complicity in the death. Our religion believes that an enemy causes all death, and hence, after death, the first action is to cut off a portion of the dead man's garment and keep it for the diviner who will search the cause of death. The relatives keep the burial place secret or is guarded for seven days, lest an enemy digs up the corpse and use it for witchcraft. Today, when we bury our dead, the senior boy is taught a ritual where he murmurs over the grave of his parent as he throws the first clout of

soil on the coffin. he says, "You can rest in peace, do not trouble us, i will give you all that you want." Shaving the heads of all the relatives marks the period of mourning, or a black band is tied on the right arm near the shoulder. This is continued until the cause of death is known and avenged by the diviner.

Mthwakazi religion believes that it is imperative that death be reported to the ancestral spirit and that the spirits be satisfied because unless so, more troubles or deaths may follow as many of these, we believe, occur when the spirits are unhappy, and they allow enemies to punish us. For these ties to be maintained a bull is kept in the kraals of every head of family, upon which the ancestral spirits are embodied. Those living in cities today use large cylindrical highly polished stones embedded in the front of the house. Black goats represent the spirits of women. In the houses of the male members of the lineage, individuals keep spears. The women keep iron or copper rings or miniature hoes attached to a stick as decorations in their rooms. Above all this human belief and representation, the religion believes in other hosts whose powers are less defined in form and character. There are mountain spirits, which we believe if you see, you die. Rivers are said to be full of other hosts of spirits represented by big snakes of which some fly. The greatest and most shadowy of the spirits Mthwakazi believes in is the mysterious supreme being, elusive and monotheistic deity. This one is associated with all creation, and we believe he lives in the heavens. We associate him with the rainmaker; lightning and any thunderous noise is his voice. We believe if you see him, you die straight away. all other spirits, dead or alive, pay homage to a supreme being. When missionaries came, they found us anchored in this supreme being. There are rocks, big trees, shrines, and pools where we send our diviners to mediate for the nation. When there are problems of illnesses, drought, or wars, our diviners go to meet our god at these places. Our culture, our education, our trade, all we believe, come from this supreme being. it was easy for

robert Moffart and david livingstone to win believers to christ because the people of Mthwakazi had such a belief in a god unknown until the missionaries revealed him to us. In the seventeenth century, the word of the true god had reached southern africa, and in the nineteenth century, King Mzilikazi gave permission to robert Moffat to begin schools, and our religion and his preaching of Jesus agreed in many ways. Today the christian culture and Mthwakazi religion have blended very well. The king told Moffat that he could teach the people but should not teach to convert the king. Our culture and our way of living, as well as our belief in the supreme being, make us welcome christianity very easily and well.

CHAPTER ONE

BELIEFS AND THE CONCEPT OF GOD

The religious system of Mthwakazi can be taught and understood effectively under taboos, customs, dreams, omens, and spirits. Spirits are viewed as good or bad; ancestral spirits are the spirits of our dead, those who are no longer living with us in flesh, but we believe they are with us in soul and spirit. We also believe they are with our creator, the supreme being. in our midst, there are bad spirits that deal with witchcraft and wizardry; they are considered enemies of the society. The custodians of our beliefs begin in the home, the family, the community, and eventually, the chief or the king in a kingdom like our society had before we were colonized by the british in 1893. Each home has shamans or diviners who teach and uphold our religion. Our faith is based upon the origin of life, where we deal with the past often known through history; the present, which we live and can experience; and we contemplate a future and probabilities we believe by faith and hope shall be fulfilled the way we plan. The future is a continuous adventure into the unknown. The diviners, our culture, our dreams, and our faith keep us hopeful. We create reasonable probabilities and a determination of seeing a tomorrow we will live to see. This is only realized by people of faith who know, once born, you will live to see some fulfillment of some future made for us in the days to come. We, therefore, trust our spirits, our supreme being, that we can say we believe; we feel sure that our objectives, plans, and achievements will be undertaken someday. Mthwakazi's belief and faith make us live a life with hope, knowing we are what we are because there is a spirit that drives our lives. The relationship between this spirit and the living must be maintained, and certain standards must be upheld, and respect for the ones gone must be accorded. however small a belief may be, to the people of Mthwakazi, it influences life as we also believe that faith and beliefs are like molds or guides that shape the nation. The younger minds must be shaped at early ages because they shape well and easily while still green. Once they are missed at tender ages, it will be difficult to make them observe the fabric of the society. Mthwakazi, therefore, endeavor to set trainers and teachers at all levels to make the youth realize that a bad life will follow you to your graves. They must also know, by their way of living, they not only offend their family heads, but they also offend the spirits and, eventually, offend our supreme being.

The trainers and teachers study seriously to be able to interpret small marks like birthmarks and shades of hair. They know the future of the nation is in their hands. Preparing these youngsters to respect their elders is to prepare them for adaptability into the community and into the world too. The signs that can be read and given meaning to influence you as an individual include spots on ones foot; if these are black, it indicates that your spouse will come from afar; if the black spot be on the hand, you will marry from the local community. We call these black spots *umuzi*, which means home. The whole belief of Mthwakazi people in spirits needs to be appreciated from the involvement of god, the creator, in general and the ancestral spirits in particular. There is a difference between the spirit of god and the ancestral spirit because *uNkulunkulu*, the great one, is the first and the creator of *uNhlanga*, the father of the tribe or the nation, or *uMdabuko*, the beginning. We believe the king was created and that a tribe or a nation is an offspring of one man and all our tribes acknowledge one god. From god, the creator, each nation has one king who acknowledges one ancestral spirit, *idlozi*, for each nation. We believe a country like britain has one god, the almighty, who is the god of the universe, but their king at death becomes their british ancestral spirit who will mediate between god the creator and the british people. When our king dies in Mthwakazi, he becomes our ancestral spirit who mediates for Mthwakazi people, which has nothing to do with the british. *Idlozi* is the spirit of the dead father or mother and will mediate for the living. Mthwakazi also calls *idlozi "izinyoka,"* which means snakes. These spiritual snakes procure or bestow blessings on the living. They protect the nation; they bring health and wealth to the families. These can be divided into two groups: those recent dead known to us and those long gone. The recent are considered active, involved with us more than the fourth generation spirits behind the scenes. The connection between the living and god, the creator, is done through the seniors in the village. in each home, the spirit is placed upon a beast. As need be, the family may have another beast; the community may have a shrine and a national shrine under the king. at the shrine, a shaman is put in charge to mediate for the nation under the jurisdiction of the king. The king is answerable to the unseen creator of the universe.

Mthwakazi religion and beliefs are kept and upheld through customs, omens, and taboos. These are taught orally from father to son and from mother to daughter, and they help us keep and uphold our religion and beliefs. Annually, family, community, and tribal seminars are held at which master teachers and trainers go through programs with different levels of students on our religion blended in our customs, taboos, and omens. Young people go through these lessons stage by stage until they go up the ladder of learning. This may take many years, but the system is no child left behind. In groups, men teachers train boys, while women take the girls. In groups, they undergo training in tribal beliefs, religious beliefs, and national customs and ideologies. This makes them realize who they are and what part they will take in nation building. Year after year, the fast ones integrate quickly and take their roles in the society as citizens of their homes, families, communities, and nation. Along the customs of lineage, the elder children are needed to master these trainings because they should be responsible for their homes after their parents are gone. Among the trainees, future teachers are identified and further coaching is done upon these for national jobs. Such children are pride to their parents and will be assets for the nation. Failures are shame to their parents, community, and tribe, although Mthwakazi never throws children away. We have no idea of prisons in our midst; we believe in corrective punishment on the job or on training. We also believe humans change for the better, not for the worse. The respect for parents and children is universal; hence, children belong to the nation. They can be reprimanded by any parent anywhere at any time. Mthwakazi takes any elder to be a role model for all young people who will respect the elders without question, just as they would to their parents. Teaching and giving advice, therefore, saturate the whole nation of Mthwakazi. It is true in our belief when we say wisdom is crying in the streets or in the market square; we mean we can share it and shape our people. A lot of impromptu lessons go on as life goes on, like at work. There is acquisition of wisdom and learning from all adults and from one another. On magico-medicine, we believe that the student must impress the spirit before it can choose him to inherit the art or craft. The student must show respect for all that pertains to the craft—the medium, the dress, the utensils, the duties—and, at the end of the training, must pay a token so that he will not forget the bushes he was shown and be able to mix these properly. When the community has seconded a few young ones to the shaman for training, which may take up to three years, the *sangoma* teaches them, practically involving them in digging for the roots, pounding the leaves, mixing the stuff, and the student accumulates the knowledge as life goes. Sometimes the students are in the fields of *inyanga*, tested to see how they cope with hardships. Most of the teaching here is to produce one who will also be an instructor in the near future; hence, attention and diligence are of importance on the part of the student.

Mthwakazi religion is taught, and its custodians are part of the home, the family, and the community. They teach what they live and uphold the standards that they themselves demonstrate. This teaching is not done for a living but is part of their calling in life. They do this to glorify the supreme being. Like the levites in the Jewish religion, great shamans support the king, being the head of the nation and custodian of our beliefs. Through these shamans, the king communicates with the supreme being on behalf of his kingdom and nation. Before the king can declare war against any neighbor, the shamans must be consulted to advise from the point of view of the spirits. Many from across the nation will gather at the palace and cast lots to peer into the issue to be able to predict the result of the war before the attack is done. The soldiers will be prepared in *muti* (herbal medicine) for courage and charm. if it is for defense, a lot of supplication is done to realize where the nation went wrong to be punished by a siege. a lot of sacrifices are given; blood, beer, and snuff are used to appease the spirits to help avoid any catastrophes. These gifts are taken to the national shrine to consult with the great spirit of the land and surrender to the will of the supreme being. Because of how the people of Mthwakazi respect the human blood when people die for whatever reason, the *sangoma* is consulted to search for the causes of death. in an epidemic, a drought, and a war, the doctors must search for the cause so that such must not repeat. Generally, Mthwakazi religion believe all problems can be avoided if we keep away from annoying our ancestral spirits as these may remove the defense fences of the nation that we find ourselves in problems with. Although Mthwakazi religion seems to deal more with the spirits of the ones gone to influence our lives today; we worry much about the future, which is a venture into the unknown; the determination of which only depends on our faith. in our plans, each day can be lived responsibly to expect reasonable probabilities, looking forward in faith and belief in our spirits that are sitting before the supreme supplicating on our behalf. The more we have faith, the more we live positive lives here on this land of the living. Mthwakazi faith agrees with the scriptures and does not give room for doubts because these doubts prevent and obstruct our blessings. There are elements in us which make it difficult for us to live without faith in the great spirit, either the ancestral or the supreme; hence, the relationship between the spirits and the living is significant, and certain standards of living must be maintained to keep innocent in the eyes of our ancestors. Our social interactions count a great deal. To be able to be in accord with these standards and follow them, Mthwakazi uses customs, taboos, and omens because we did not write we could not treasure these anywhere else.

CHAPTER TWO

MTHWAKAZI CUSTOMS AND BELIEFS (IMIKHUBO)

Customs, practices common to a people of a particular place, are repeatedly practiced until we habitually do them, yet they form a social habit acceptable to a people and a nation. Most of these are usually unwritten but repeatedly practiced for generations and have established a way of life. In Mthwakazi, our customs are now convictions that regulate our social life. Our religion can be studied and taught very well and effectively through our customs. These help our people keep our beliefs, and they help cement our religious beliefs as they make us act in an acceptable manner among our people without stress. If we do not act in line with our norms, we will find ourselves out of fashion. Customs also protect the believers from angering or enraging the spirits of the nation because these spirits lived these customs before they moved yonder.

One of the customs for the senior boys is to stand beside their father's grave on the day the father is buried. The boy will be holding his father's spear, piercing the ground to vindicate and declare his rights of being the heir of the dead man. The son becomes the head of his deceased father's home. The neighbors begin to engage him on issues as they did with his father hitherto. If his father was an *inyanga*, the boy must have been or must have undergone training long before the death of his father.

If our customs and beliefs are adhered to well, with respect, the family gets blessings as usual, and the loss of the father becomes an acceptable setback; our religion avoids greed and jealousy. The custom of spitting on the lump of soil by relatives, particularly by the senior boy, before they throw it into the grave is considered respectful and prayerful. all Mthwakazi rites have symbols attached to them that make these rites easy to understand and meaningful. It is also easy to appreciate the rites, the symbols thereof, and the act represented by the rite. We believe that this earth is a land for both sorrows and happiness. We trust that by appeasing our gone spirits, we expect blessings and happiness, but by enraging them, we attract hardships. Mthwakazi people endure to please their ancestral spirits, looking to someone above the living to protect and to guide the nation and to provide for our needs. This custom at the grave loosens the bitterness that the father might have had in or during his illness. We believe we show him who to deal with among those still living.

Another of the many important customs is the marriage custom. This must be obeyed from as early as courtship begins because soon after the couple begins dating, their relatives must know it. The boy is introduced to an aunt, and the girl must be known by one of the uncles. if their affair is a serious one, the aunt plays a big role in instructing the couple as to how to go about it. Under normal circumstances, the boy initiates, and the girl accepts. The boy tells his uncle who informs the family. After discussions with the relevant leadership of the boy's family, a gobetween is sent to the girl's family through the person instructed by the aunt. The go-between will announce the request to marry their daughter. The girl's family accepts the word but will send the messenger empty-handed, instructing him to carry word that they will have to wait on them as they need time to consider it. They need to consult with their daughter and the leadership of the family. During the consultations with the girl, the aunt does a thorough investigation to find out if the girl is still in good standing or else she may be carrying. if she is pregnant, the normal custom of marrying initiated by the boy's family changes to the one the girl's family rolls the ball first. An aunt, together with the girl, will tell the boy to warn his family of their visit to come and bring umthwalo wakhe (his burden), as we describe it in our custom, bringing his burden to his parents. All this is done in prayers to the ancestral spirits. It is a shame for a girl to fail to marry and yet brings an unclaimed child at home. On the day the aunt brings the girl and finds the boy's family waiting for them, that is when good shall come out of this arrangement. Always, pre-arrangements are done so that no part of the deal is caught unaware. The young guy will know when the girl and the aunt are coming and warn his family who will be ready to meet them, ready too with all what is needed at such circumstances. When the aunt arrives, discussions quickly take place because if they are unwelcome, they may depart soon after few exchanges. The boy's family will have called most of the boys into the room, just as a matter of procedure, and the girl must identify the one responsible, and the rest go away while the culprit remains. If he accepts responsibility and that he wants to marry, then there are nominal payments, which are known customary from both families, this being part of our Venda magico-religion; these payments are believed to be universal in Mthwakazi. To be refused by the guy is an embarrassment for a girl and a shame to her family, especially her mother. It is, therefore, relief and victory for both the aunt and girl to be accepted. The universal payments in this case include an amount of cash that the boy gives the girl through the aunt to buy maternity clothes ingewayo, a goat that is brought and shown to the aunt before being slaughtered for their relish during their stay at the boy's home. The head of the goat, the skin, and the legs are kept as they will be taken by the aunt as proof that the boy is responsible and that he is willing to marry the girl. Customary, if you see the aunt come back carrying those items, then you know the girl has been accepted for marriage. They can stay for at least three days and then depart to take the report back. Thereafter, arrangements for marriage can go along the normal procedure. The idea behind the goatskin being taken by the girl's family is that the skin will be a baby carrier when the child is born.

The procedure of marriage when the girl is not pregnant is through the boy's family messenger who is sent from the boy's side. The custom is to negotiate between the two families for our children to marry. The go-between shall be directed to the person responsible in the girl's family who will take his or her time to put the plan down for the two families to meet. When they eventually meet, it is the girl's parents who either accept or refuse the marriage deal. In our customs, although they are changing slightly now, the father of the girl may decide for the daughter as to whom she should marry. When the deal is accepted, a meeting is arranged where discussions center on the dowry, and our customs say much of this comes from the boy's family to the girl's family. Very little goes to the girl because most of the payments here are to appease the parents so that, in turn, they ask the ancestral spirits to bless this marriage and the new couple. Mthwakazi customs and religion are happy for the new couple when they have children then the rest of the charges may then be paid. We believe in procreation more than just husband and wife. In payment of the dowry, that will include a few beasts and cash, and one of the beasts must be for the girl's mother (Inkomo Yohlanga). how this marriage custom is taught or enforced depends on the aunts and uncles. When a marriage is being negotiated, the families do it openly and practically and aim at training and teaching those who have become of age. It is so inclusive that many family members find themselves doing something. Always, when such events occur in the home, a selected team led by a senior will include a few understudies. More will be dealt with when marriages are proposed and weddings arranged and carried out. We will see here that community leaders are trained to handle engagements, home marriage, divorce, and childbearing and caring.

CHAPTER THREE

OMENS (IMHLOLO)

Mthwakazi people believe in omens as part of our religion. Whereas omens can be generally those of our religion are universal. These are signs that when seen or when it occurs predict a happening to come. They are warnings that form part of our religion on our dayto-day living. in our religion, we regard them as prophetic signs and are associated with the behavior of nature around us. Animals, birds, reptiles, or vegetation may warn or can give prediction to travelers. Because omens are universal in Mthwakazi, they can be grouped into two types: those that predict good happenings and those that predict bad things. As Mthwakazi religion believes that the recently dead guard or police the homes and families of the living, we believe they do so by using animal, plants, and any symbols to reveal to us our immediate dangers, misfortunes, perils, happiness, and securities. Belief in omens is stronger in country areas than in urban centers because of the abundance of animal presence and vegetation upon which omens are associated. Omens are so blended in our society that they control our day-to-day living. These make the people so careful to recognize any unusual movement of animals or plants.

The teaching of how and what each sign means is done practically by involvement and as we lead our life generally. For example, while walking to the fields, a son alerts his father of a rat darting across the pathway in their front or an earthworm burrowing a hole; the father tells his son that the sign warns them or announces the death of a relative. They are required to turn back and tell the family of the omen, and the whole family keeps anticipating the news of death. It may take time before they hear of it, but they will have been warned; the family is prepared beforehand. Those animals that do not live or dig holes when seen doing so, it is, therefore, a sign of death. Animals, like chameleons, seen digging a hole in the ground is a sign of death. it is unusual; hence, we associate this with death. Chameleons keep the color of the place they are hiding in, but if it just turns its color because it saw you, again, this is a sign of death. To see a sand snake foretells good luck or a safe journey. To travelers, to hear the chirping of birds in the bush denotes that the traveler is safe from wild animals. Our religion teaches that we must always be watchful for unusual behavior of animals and read what it may mean as we do not take anything for granted.

When a branch falls in your sight, breaking from the main tree, this denotes death of an important person in the community. For doves or pigeons to perch on the roof of your house, it foretells good gain, unless the pigeons seem all sick, and they are yours, then they report that there would be illness in the home. Bad omens are those from bad birds, like crows, vultures, and owls, because we believe these birds are companions of witches, and they denote hardships when seen flying over one's home. A python hears you first before you are able to see it, and under natural circumstances, it will stretch and lie still until you pass, but if it carries on wriggling away, then this is a bad omen that denotes bad luck. To see cats mating at daylight in the home foretells untold hardships, danger, or loss of life. The howling of a female dog stooping with its back at you is a warning sign of mourning, and if it does it at daytime in the home means death may occur to a close relative. When cockerels fight in the home, you must expect a very important stranger, or you will receive good news. Mthwakazi community believes that the stars and the moon reveal the condition of the nation's heath that period. The new moon's position may foretell good heath or foretell illnesses and mishappenings. The nation will be forewarned. A shooting star at night reveals plenty and good luck for one who sees it, yet a tailed shooting star denotes bad luck. Generally, omens in Mthwakazi beliefs are occurrences or phenomena believed to usher future happenings. The teaching of these omens to our people is done as life proceeds and is done from father to son and from mother to daughter. There are many omens that affect us more by sex hence those that deal with boys much more than with the girls. You will soon realize that our religion is learned and mastered through seeing and doing. The teachers or trainers are our own and are always with the trainees, influencing them by their way of living. Among the quick juniors, the senior trainers will be looking for some who can be made trainers in the near future. Mthwakazi's education has always succeeded alongside formal education.

CHAPTER FOUR

GENERAL TABOOS (AMAZILO)

Generally, a taboo to the Mthwakazi people is a prohibition or a forbiddance to profane, use, or contact with on grounds of morality. This regards things considered dangerous or supernatural or having supernatural powers. It is a banned act to avoid risks; hence, you may not touch, you may not say, you may not look for fear of immediate harm from a supernatural force. In the story of lot's wife, she had been told what was forbidden, that was to look back and see sodom and gomorrah on fire; hence, she suffered the penalty from a supreme power. To Mthwakazi, it is taboo for one to look back. Taboos, in Mthwakazi, are imposed by social customs or by a protective measure. The people, in their belief of taboos, may separate them with symbols of ritualistic nature. Taboos play a great deal in mastering many of our teachings, as they are a motivator, like the idea of a stick and carrot. By doing right, we believe we get blessings from our ancestors, and this is easy when we adhere to the taboos that guide us in our lives. Mthwakazi's faith is the key to most of our way of interaction because whatever we believe about the origin and destiny of our life is based on mere faith. Our faith in this is seen on how easy it is to respond to a name given at birth. All of us take the names we are given and hold on to them just by faith. Whereas we deal with the past, the present, the future that concerns us more, we only hold upon our faith and hope. Our thoughts and actions are to be directed and controlled by a belief in some power that is bigger. Taboos then help us create survival routines by which our actions are found good without strain. The spirit of our ancestor mediates between our creator and us. If the relationship between the dead and the living is to be realized, a standard of living guided by a code of ethics must be maintained. Because this is always accorded to the spirit of the dead, such as taboos are taught to our nation as guidelines.

In Mthwakazi, certain snakes are symbols of the presence of the ancestral spirits. It is taboo to kill or molest snakes like the green mamba and the sand snake. Green snakes are connected to the spirit of the ones gone. When these are seen at the home, they are considered to be our dead ones who have come to visit. To see any of these snakes is lucky as they foretell good fortunes. They are associated with good health and prosperity. The Inyandezulu is a green snake connected to all Mthwakazi people and most of those who came from Zululand and south africa. it is considered a royal pet and should be allowed the freedom of the palace. It heralds good news, health and prosperity to the nation. Killing these snakes is disconnecting the spirits of the dead from the living. Mthwakazi believes these snakes are the flesh of our gone ones coming to visit and encouraging us on our faith in the creator who is our maker.

Hence, it is taboo to kill these snakes. The teaching and training of taboos is done practically by those who have been coached already by prohibiting juniors killing these snakes when they appear in our homes. What is interesting is the snakes rarely bite us unless molested or we also believe, unless sent to warn us, to repent from our wrongdoings like what happened in israel in the wilderness. When this happens, the snake is killed with snuff and burned, and then it will go back to whosoever sent it to you to bewitch.

The snake taboos are the ones connected to the supernatural, like the first three of the Ten commandments, and yet there are those taboos that connect us together as people of a nation. It is taboo to walk backward because it is dangerous, in fact, and you may fall into a ditch or stumble on a rock. Our seniors teach this by saying if you walk backward, your mother will fall and die in a water can. If you love your mother, you will avoid this act and save yourself from injuries and, eventually, just create a habit of avoiding this. Avoid walking through graveyards because your feet will crack. It is taboo to walk though or play in graveyards, of course, for sheer respect, but we teach by a warning that one's feet will crack. Mthwakazi people wholly believe and respect the dead, and we believe they hate being trodden on as this may seem rude and may make the spirits of the dead angry and cause mishaps for the one who walks on or his family for walking upon his graves. Our beliefs also include graves as being places that harbor snakes. Graves are sacred places, but boys may not know this to avoid these places; boys are warned through taboos. all these taboos are not all very bad, but these are some that are for the good, and they need the shamans or community doctors to explain and sometimes mediate to quell the oncoming misfortune. When driving along a road and a big animal or a rare and nocturnal animal like an antibore crosses the road in front of your car, you need to stop and consider driving on or make a return because we believe it is a sign warning you of negative consequences ahead. if you have a witch doctor with you or in the neighborhood, you get to him and explain. he will deal with this and bless your way. This, we find in bible stories, when you could visit a seer to advice you on small things, including where your sheep may be found after they went astray.

Utensils common to the nation of Mthwakazi include pumpkin cups that can be used for food when fresh and as water containers when allowed to overgrow and dry, then the seeds and stuff inside are scooped, and the gourd is used as a drinking cup. It is taboo for unmarried women to eat in such cups, walking to a well to draw water, as it is believed that on their wedding day, the weather will turn cold and rainy. it is taboo for young women to walk thorough a herd of cattle grazing in the fields, more so when they are in their monocyclic days, as our culture believes the woman won't stop bleeding even after the days are over. She will have to visit a village doctor to be treated but will also be reprimanded for ignoring that taboo. Most cattle breeders in our nation treat their herds with magic that may affect these women when they go through these herds. The women may disturb the magic if they, the women, were treated for such beforehand, and the circle in the cattle production, even of milk, may be disturbed. When discovered late, this may cause quarrels in the community that may be settled at the chief's court. Such cases are said to be shameful, unwarranted, and would enrage the spirits. Such also have far-reaching results that may cause the woman to be barren and fail to have children in the future even after marrying. so to Mthwakazi, in their own rights, taboos are as important as they are to the nation of Israel.

Mothers of little children are taught that it is taboo for a child to be sat at the doorways because they won't grow as the doorway is stepped by everyone coming in or out of the hut. We believe, even if one does not step or walk over the baby but walk on the doorway, one is pressing down growth, like in the case of seeds that germinate on paths or roadways where people will tramp on the crop until it is squashed flat. There are some herbs used by people in general or in particular that are believed may retard the growth of small children; hence, they must be kept away from doorways. Water and rain are believed to be a gift from god, and when consumed, one must kneel to show respect for the rain-god. If you drink water standing, it is taboo, and we believe you anger the *Inkosazana*, the god of rain, which we believe is in lightning and, when angry, can strike and kill without mercy.

It is taboo to drag a cat with its tail as this causes blindness or sore eyes. This may be to avoid abuse of domestic animals. it is painful for you to see or hear the animal, dog or cat, cry for mercy when pulled by the tail. Some retaliate and bite you seriously; hence, to teach and develop that love for our pets, we give a prohibition covered in a taboo. It is also taboo for men, especially boys, to be seen eating from a pot. They will be hated by their bosses, and for boys, they will be cowardly and will be beaten by their peers and will be made to run all day under overwhelming instructions and commands. This taboo may just be a way of teaching the men and boys that pots are to be left to the women, so better to avoid the interference. Young women must not mend or sew their garments while wearing them because they will sew themselves from childbearing. It is taboo as the women won't have children. This teaches the dangers needles have because no matter how careful, one may prick oneself with the needle. What is interesting is the customs, omens, and taboos of the religion of Mthwakazi have moved with the modern world, indicating their way of teaching has shifted much with civilization. They cannot be considered remote. After a heavy meal and one feels constipation, one just uses a broom to sweep your stomach; the constipation goes away. When you feel sick and are about to vomit, to avoid throwing up, you sniff your armpit; the smell of it stops you from vomiting. When you sneeze, we believe you are out of danger, if you were ill. New food from fields cannot be eaten before the rite called *ukuchinsa*. Contagious diseases cause and calls for family members to be abstinence because respect for our spirits will bless the family and be healed including the land.

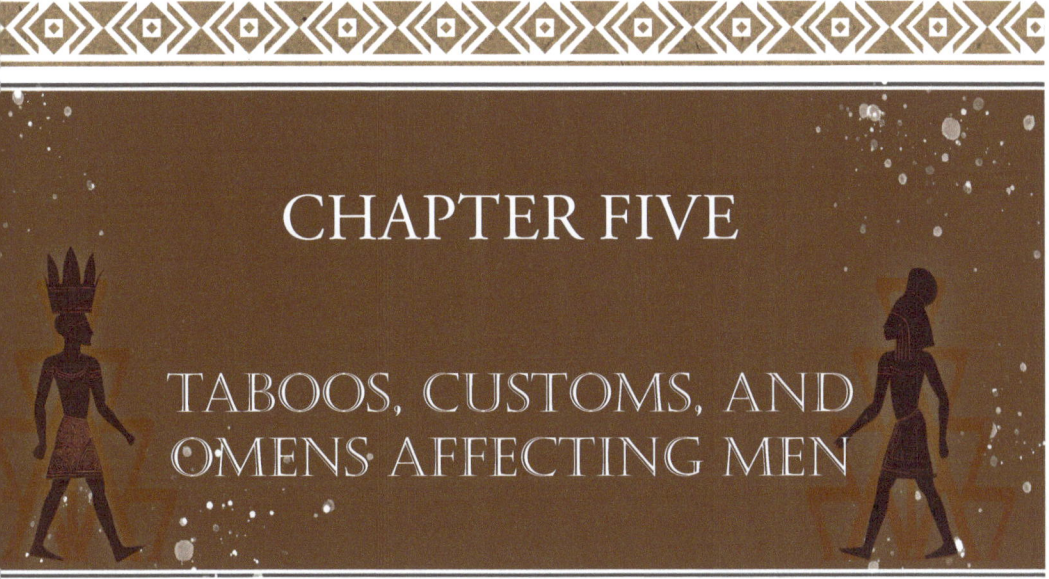

CHAPTER FIVE

TABOOS, CUSTOMS, AND OMENS AFFECTING MEN

Men have fewer taboos that affect them because men want to claim freedom more than other family members. Young men who are active and are in the army are demanded to observe purity days before they go to war. It is forbidden to go in the house with your wife until the war is over. This was like this even during the time of uriah who refused, even though King david had given him permission, but it was against man-at-war taboos to meet your wife when you were a solider at war. This is done because the medicinal or magic treatments they are given require that they abstain from sexual intercourse during the whole period of the war. The sitting on a grinding stone or stamping block without placing a stone in or under it, as it is believed, may cause the death of one's wife. This is connected with the creation and death myth to be covered later. The men are to know all the signs that forecast the future many times through omens. They understand the weather and climate and know the behavior of domesticated animals and vegetation much better than storekeeping or office work. The names and colors of cattle, shrubs, grasses, and trees are common wisdom among the men. Signs of coming events enable Mthwakazi to plan accordingly. Swallows come first, and men know these announce the rainy season. The roofs and thatches of their homes are mended accordingly. The plowing season is foretold by the shooting of tress like river willows and many others including vlei bulbs indicate for seed and all readying for plowing. If wild berries bear plenty of fruits, there is a likelihood of plenty rains and plenty harvests. Harvest ants also announce plenty rains and a bumper crop for the new season. The people of Mthwakazi believe that this earth is both a land of happiness and a land of the hardship and sorrows. More of the hardships or happiness can be foretold in our omens and avoided if we keep well our taboos.

When a boy is born in the home and happens to be the first boy, he is nurtured in such a manner that he needs to realize he will take all the responsibility of his father as head of the family just as his father passes away. The day his father is buried, he is this child, the senior boy in the family, who stands holding his family spear at the head side of his father's grave. His responsibility is respected, regardless of his age, as long as he has turned reasonable age. After he has taken over all his siblings, his mother will respect him as they did their father. All that the father used to handle is given to this boy to handle, though he may depend on his mother or uncles for advice. While growing, there are omens and taboos he must observe to be able to grow and handle as the head of family without being rejected by the family spirits. Mthwakazi believes that when everything is observed and respected, the boy will just take after his father without problems because the boy will I be shown some of the family activities and duties or responsibilities by the spirits who will visit him in dreams or in his common sense.

When growing from his mother's breast, he is taught to be with other men and to avoid the kitchen, going to the cattle kraals early in the morning even for his urinary releases. At an early age, he must be going with the goats into the bush to graze them. If he is beaten by other boys his age, he cannot report this to his parents because they may curse him for being or acting like a coward or a girl. In many groups of Mthwakazi clans and tribes, the boys are circumcised for health reasons. The Jews circumstances on circumcision were announced by god to abraham, yet though nowhere written, the people of Mthwakazi circumcise their boys; not all of their clans do so. The Venda and the Xhosa-lemba are outspoken on this custom. They believe it contributes to the future manhood of the boys. Many venereal diseases are avoided or controlled by some of these customs like circumcision.

When the boys are in the early teens, at around thirteen to sixteen years of age, they qualify to undergo this rite. During the winter season, every year or two, the teens are taken into classes in the bush under the instructors and shamans. The boys are cut away from homes and treated to be brazen and may beat up people who may pass through their hideout. They hunt wild beasts for their food and may feed on raw meat. For a month or so, they are made wild to be ready for the occasion of circumcision. The present generation uses common razor to cut the boy's foreskin, the early generations used a stone knife, and magic from the roots and leaves of known bushes are used to treat the wounds to avoid them from decomposition. The bushes are mixed with some of the flesh for them to treat these wounds, and some are eaten to restore lost blood. Because of this rite's importance among these Mthwakazi clans, the classes in the formal education schools lose attendance for the three winter months. The department of education has instructed the areas affected to ignore this problem and accept the boy's absence from school for this purpose. The chiefs and local leaders are asked to acknowledge this and warn travelers to avoid the areas. Otherwise, if they are beaten or killed, the boys may not be charged for the incidents. Instead, the intruder's family may be charged for interference. The payment for such charges are laid down within the customary package, and such is usually a beast that is paid through the chief or headman. it is slaughtered and roasted to cleanse the curse that could result from walking through an area considered sacred or set apart for the boys' circumcision. After the rite is over, the boys are allowed to join the community. They will be obviously different from what they were before, in that they will be respected quite differently. They can now be counted among adults instead of children. They can also be allowed to propose marriage. They will be allowed to take part in community decisions and can represent their clan or family in many issues affecting the nation. They become part of the teachers and trainers of their customs as most of Mthwakazi's teachings, training, and things learned are passed from senior to junior or from father to son, mother to daughter. At this age, the boys are fertile ground for the propagation of their nation's customs and life.

CHAPTER SIX

TABOOS, CUSTOMS, AND OMENS AFFECTING WOMEN

In Mthwakazi religion, the place of women and their role are clearly defined in the relationship she created when she marries. She becomes a bridge between her own family and the family of her spouse. Whereas it is the duty or obligation of the man to be a breadwinner to feed, clothe, and comfort his wife, the woman is expected to cook and bear children. She must prepare bedding, please her husband, remain faithful, and bring up their children according to customs. Obedience or subordination on the part of the woman does not in any way imply servitude but merely sustains and enhances their marriage bond. When a home has good rapport, the ancestral spirits readily bestow blessings upon the family and its members.

Many of those taboos and omens or customs that affect the women are most important during pregnancy because the seed in her must begin to relate with or be identified with the rest of its living ones. The early stages of pregnancy are usually kept secret to avoid an enemy interfering with the unborn child. The ancestral spirits must be told about the pregnancy first and be involved to protect it against the witches who are believed to take their jobs easier at early stages. There is a belief among Mthwakazi people in our religion that the embryo can be a wonderful medico-magic when killed still in its mother's womb. This can be used for positive results or for dangerous results because we believe the embryo is just a spirit, not yet polluted by the flesh. These are considered angels so innocent but can be misguided missiles. The pregnant woman will be advised not to eat meat of the totem animal of the father because we believe if she did, the unborn child's health may be impaired, which may cause deformity of limbs, retardation in growth, or feebleness. Disobeying may cause mental diseases in the child in later days to come. Falling of teeth is also associated to the woman eating the meat of the totem animal during her pregnancy. It is of utmost importance for the mother during gestation and nursing periods to be very careful and act responsibly so that she does not carry the blame. She must avoid or be faithful all that period because we believe any extra marital activities are a great curse to the unborn child. If she doubts who the man is who made her pregnant, there is no dna test, but what she is taught is to give the man water to bath his body or face then treacherously drink that dirty water, then the child will resemble the man or one of his family members.

Many Mthwakazi families rear cattle and make sure that they calf. Otherwise, every year a fertility rite is used (iziko). This is believed to be very powerful that it may cause instant abortion or intermittent periodical flow. Women are taught that it is taboo for them to cross through a herd of cattle, which is merely a magical practice that has nothing to do with the spirits, although the ancestors are told all fertility rites to assist and protect the animals. The woman's attitude toward the procreation phenomenon underlines her important duty and role of molding and nourishing the new member, from the womb to childhood.

Whereas polygamy in the culture of Mthwakazi was acceptable in their religion for men, it was shameful for a woman to have more than one husband. This reduces her dignity to that of a prostitute. In the early days, the act had a capital penalty. This was not regarded unfair when men were allowed many wives. It was considered acceptable, even by our ancestors who believed our creator granted this to abraham too when sarah asked him to make children with haggar, the slave woman. The man was considered the seed of the totem and cocreator with *uMdali*. In our cultural magico-religion, prosperity, riches, even human resources were attributed to men. Jacob was the father of twelve sons from four women, the sons who today form the twelve tribes of israel. God blessed this nation; hence, the religion of Mthwakazi believes in what our god, the supreme, called upon abraham, isaac, and Jacob, that men are the offspring of all humanity; a woman is part of her children. When a woman carrying a calabash of water met someone who was thirsty and needed a drink, she was to place the calabash of water on the ground for the man to help himself; it was taboo for the woman to allow the man to draw with a cup from her head. This was, or even today, regarded as drawing her fertility away. Many families have fertility rites in their fields, and women, especially when carrying or in their monthly days, were forbidden from walking across such fields as the fertility rite would cause intermittent blood flow continuously until a doctor attended to her. If carrying the fetus would be spoiled, these mishaps may cause permanent and severe complications that may result in sterility in future. Women are forbidden to cross fields and/or herds of grazing cattle. The old ladies in the families took this seriously and made these as lessons and part of their curriculum in the teaching they give to the girls when the girls grow into puberty.

Through the ages of growth, women develop physically and are put under the watchful eyes of their mentors. When young women begin to develop breasts, they are trained how to keep themselves clean, and when they are at puberty and begin moving to adolescence and into womanhood, when in many cases they find themselves arrogant and rude, the mentors work hard on this group because it is a period of character formation. It is also during these stages in girls' lives that they develop resistance and complacency, that teaching and training make very little progress, and many get spoiled in way of character and, eventually, become problems in community in future. it becomes a shame not only to the family but also to the community and the nation as a whole; hence, such teachers are required in our religion. At this stage, boys develop muscles and deep voices. Mentors take them at random for hunting game fishing and just those activities that make them aware of being breadwinners. In the forest and bush, they are shown roots and herbs they need to chew so that they may develop hard skin and some that help in the formation of sperms and thus aid to full puberty. At the entry into puberty and experiencing of their first menstruation, most girls cry. Mothers know what to do when their daughters report of this happening. The mother takes red bitter corn or sweet-reed seeds *izimba* or *imfe*; these are ground and made into meal that is mixed with soot, *isinyayi*, and boiled and stirred into porridge for the girl to eat. When done well, this is a treatment for the pains that comes with these periods. After a year or so in puberty, a celebration is held in the village for these girls who found themselves in that stage of growth. neighbors are invited to this special dance for the girls that have crossed into puberty. Younger ones too are included for the dance, which goes on through the night. Those who will have turned the age of puberty sit in the center of the crowd as their parents and the invited eat and drink at the celebration. The following morning, the girls go to the river to take a bath and come back to continue the celebrations until sunset when they disperse to their homes. In some harsh communities, others may attack them with switches before they disperse and while naked. This is done to harden her in anticipation of marrying a bad husband who will beat them time after time. It is a lesson for the future in marriage.

To these girls, lessons on to be good housewives, care of children, behavior toward men, use of sex, and cookery begin at home and in the family. The old ladies who know the village craft engage her in a variety of cores. Central to all these teachings was that she must master one art or craft that may become her trade in future. This is usually what her mother mastered and is part of what she got involved in at an early age. In our religion, it is a requirement that a woman presents a nice basket to her husband at the day of marriage as a declaration to him that she has become his wife. Mthwakazi forbids sex before marriage; whoever does it is treated with scorn. It is at such training sessions that girls are taught faithfulness because if this is not upheld, the girl will be looked down upon and despised by the village members. After the puberty rite celebrations, special lessons are given on regulation on sex desires to the girls. During childhood, when the children are still on breastfeed, mothers are taught that if they squeezed drops of milk into the child's genitals, the madness for sex is reduced. This treatment, Mthwakazi believes, helps the girls, in particular, to control their impulses for sex even under pressure. Omens affect both gender at almost the same degree, and we believe they are signs from our recent gone ones. The spirits will be patrolling the home and family using animal symbols to reveal to the recipients the immediate misfortunes, perils, dangers, as well as revealing possible fortunes, happiness, and security in gains. Omens are national and easy to divide them into bad or good omens. Mthwakazi's belief in omens is so strong that in rural areas, where animals are many, omens are blended into our society that they eventually control the day-to-day activities of the individuals, causing at times unnecessary confusion and despondencies. For example, a woman on her way to fetch water at the river sees an earthworm burrowing a hole in the pathway; she believes it warns of death. By our belief, she has to stop going to the river and get back home and warn the rest of a possible death in the home. This is taken seriously that the family will wait on it, yet it may not be until a few days or so. Bad omens affect the individual's mind and operations and dependent upon how that society upholds omens. Reptiles, like chameleons, gray cobras, and cats also mating at daytime in the home signal death and untold hardships. For a woman, expecting an eagle or hawk flying over her head denotes good heath during the time of her pregnancy. it may also indicate that the child will be a boy and that he will be warlike, tough just like the eagle. If you see a wasp flying around you and your body, this warns of hateful enemies meeting about you. if it stings you, then your enemies will triumph over you, but if it does not sting you, this will be just a warning that you must be watchful. Witches and wizards are more active when you are pregnant and during funerals, yet omens are also surrounding us at these times; we need to be watchful at those times. Like modern science, witches and wizards love to use fetus and believe this is very useful in their medicines when killed before birth. Omens play a major role in connecting the dead and gone ones to the living. Mthwakazi religion upholds this connection and truly believes one, once born, never dies but only translates into a spirit that lives forever with our creator and connects with its own through omens and dreams.

CHAPTER SEVEN

MARRIAGE AND CHILDBEARING

In Mthwakazi religion and culture, much respect is given to men who have many wives, as their kraals are big and famous. The man becomes a man and dignified as his kraal grows in way of wives and children. The spirit of oneness and unity must prevail in the home, if peace and order and good life were maintained in the kraal. Harmonious relations and unity are results of respect for one another. Men are regarded as men provided they are able to keep their big kraals under good relations and unity among family members, more so if this unity transcends through and among even daughters-in-law. The grandchildren need to respect their seniors as they respect themselves. The ancestral spirits also help in such big homes and families. We find this even in countries like usa, in the Mormon sects. Mthwakazi believe it is biblical to marry more than one wife. Adultery is punishable by severe penalties, although in cases of impotence, a younger brother from the same mother may be authorized to get children for his brother. The impotent brother may not be told of the arrangement. This was done to keep peace and unity and to also cool down the woman, hence she strays. If he realizes it, old women are sent to advise him.

The father or the head of the family takes charge and initiates the activities of the kraal. Some of his sons may implement their decisions, and this is how they are trained for the future, when they will find themselves heads too and running their kraals. The father settles disputes and offers a water libation to spirits, if there be illness in the home, especially if the illness is believed to be due to the anger of the spirits of the ancestors. The first wife is responsible for the distribution of the food and clothing. All the man gets must be given to the senior wife for determination. She must be fair and must know her responsibility must be beyond reproach. She calls the junior wives, and they come into her presence with respect, and they kneel, receive the articles, then thank the father, although he will not be there, then thank the senior wife and go. She raises the tone of the family by her sense of judgment and boosts its morale by exercising justice and fair play to all the members of the family, regardless of differences experienced in the family because most of the women come from different backgrounds and must be blended together through the father, the senior wife, the elder sons, and the grandchildren. The belief is that the ancestral spirits oversee the kraal and would be hurt if there be misunderstanding in the family. at meal times, men eat together by peers and age, while women go and eat at the senior wife's hut. Food is brought from different kitchens to a men's center where they meet and chat, discussing family issues, training the future leaders of the family. They eat from the same plate at a time as the plates are replaced when empty, and plates come one after the other until all are done.

In choosing a spouse, tribalism is always practiced among Mthwakazi people because of the role played by ancestral spirits in the home, among other issues. Our beliefs, our customs, and our language used by indwelling spirit (*idlozi*) can easily break a marriage bond between spouses whose cultures and spiritual beliefs differ from each other. Related groups of clans have similar spirits, which obey when a water libation is offered them. This does not mean that all is well when you marry from the same clan. We endeavor to lead good lives in marriages because that makes us prosperous as we please our ancestral spirits.

A dube cannot marry a dube, but when a woman is married, she immediately grafts accordingly so that she, thereafter, adopts the gods of the home in which she will live the rest of her life. The significance of this grafting is realized when at her symbolic death, the man's rite is used at her burial. This reveals that the spirit of the home accepts the woman and is very important in homemaking. When Mr. dube marries Ms. ndlovu, she gives up her gods and is absorbed into the dube family so that even if she falls ill, she cannot call upon her former family spirits to intervene, except if her spirits want her to be an *inyanga*, which will still be paid for by the dube family through what we call *ukukhunga*, and the spirit of the ndlovu family will release her to the dubes as an *inyanga* that will live at its marriage home.

The personality and disposition of the man counts a great deal in marriage proposals. The man's status regulated or is a pointer or is suggestive as to how the procedure of the negotiations will lead. In cases where the man is poor, generally, the woman will bring some of her assets to cushion and make a foundational start for their fledgling home. She can bring a few herds. Commonly, it is the man who must pay *lobolo*, which, to Mthwakazi people, is not regarded as an asset and is not given priority or ever mentioned at any stage of the marriage preparations. However, if the woman gives children to the man, it becomes a duty of the man to give his in-laws a hoe, cattle, or goats as a token of appreciation for what the woman is doing for him. The amount or number of cattle are not specified; it all depends on what the man thinks is a reasonable gift. *Lobola* is paid to have custody of your children because, customarily, the children belong to the wife's parents until the man pays *lobolo*. Because of this custom, the man may not ask for *lobolo* for his daughter from a guy who intends to marry his daughter until he, the man, pays his wife, the mother to the daughter. At worst cases, the guy proposing to marry our daughter may be asked to pay *lobolo* that will straight away be taken by the grandparents of my daughter. This is no longer considered just *lobolo* but compensation, which sounds shameful for a man to allow it to take place after a generation in marriage, unless he is not fit to work and have his own property to be able to settle his ways with his in-laws before the children are grown to marry. To avoid such shame, the in-laws have allowed some of their property to accumulate and be considered the man's, although it was brought by the woman at marriage; hence, most of the calves born in the in-laws' custody may be accounted to him just as Jacob and laban in the old Testament.

The process for marriage in Mthwakazi has shifted drastically, but it was not the guy who determined the outcome of the settlement because the parents were not obligated to comply with their daughter's choice, because the father reserved the right to divert the wedding to a man of his choice, even if the man was years older than the girl. When the two, that is the boy and the girl, think they are ready to marry, procedures are arranged under the guidance of aunties and uncles to follow what is right according to Mthwakazi customs that we believe please the ancestral spirits. If the woman is already carrying, indicating there was sexual relations before marriage, instead of the man sending a go-between, the girl's family sends an aunt with the girl to the man's family to announce the pregnancy. These arrangements are done with both families aware, and the rites are followed accordingly. On the day of the aunt and girl's visit to the man's home, the boy's family prepare for all the reception. The way it is done will be indicative as to whether the marriage will be carried on or it will be a failure.

If the boy accepts responsibility, he makes ready money for her maternity dress, *ingcayo*; ready with a goat for the aunt's relish during her visit; some of which will be taken back to the girl's family that must include the goat's skin and its head. These are the rites that show the boy is willing to marry the girl and accepts responsibility of the pregnancy. The skin is considered, in Mthwakazi, to be the baby carrier when the baby finally arrives. The head is just to show or indicate the size of the goat, which expressed the appreciation by the boy's family, especially the boy himself, for his girl's visit and choice for him as her future husband. When the aunt arrives, a meeting is called where all the possible boys at the home are called and included in the initial discussions. They come in and listen when the aunt is presenting her case and her mission with the girl. An uncle on the boy's side responds by showing all the boys in their family and asks the girl to identify the one she claims to be responsible for her pregnancy. Once that is done, the rest are free to go, and the one indicated remains to account and accept and promise before his uncles and the girl's aunt as witnesses. The rest of the reception rite follows, and a goat is brought in and shown to the aunt who will give them, the in-laws, a go-ahead to slaughter the goat and do all the necessary procedures. Then follows celebrations with eating and drinking; also, this is when the spirits are told that their grandchild is espousing.

After this meeting and rite, the family allows the aunt to take the girl back to go and give a report and show the articles of appreciation. It will then be the girl's family to initiate the next steps; the boy's side waits on them. The meeting at which the aunt will report and the sight of the articles she brought will straight be indicative of the way of things to those who are versed in our religion. If she was impressed, she makes sure she impresses her own to read the success of the whole thing because the family members will take from where she leaves. A date will be arranged where and when the two families will meet. The girl is instructed to inform the boy to let his family know of the date when they will be needed to meet. To the girl, the pending in-laws are referred to as "your people," *abantu bakho.* The boy's side chooses a spokesperson who will negotiate on their behalf. He is the leader of the delegation and must be versed in the customs and cultures of marriages. He must be aware of the diversities too between the families that are arranging this marriage. In the delegation, the boy may be among them. At this meeting, the discussion will revisit the issue from when the aunt took it up. Arrangements then go on, and relationships are began and cemented. These relationships include charges and payments in the case of breaking the family law to the extent of having their daughter pregnant before marriage proposals. Mthwakazi has a charge called *uthango*, which we believe the boy was breaking when he sneaked into the girl's home at odd times without permission from the girl's family. This is just a way of guessing that the boy came into our home and broke the home's fence or border rules. For the one already pregnant, some groups of tribes charge what they call "damages," that you are considered to have damaged their daughter when you had sex with her outside or before marriage proposals. These charges and payments are not according to how big the amounts are, but the ideas behind them are more important than their value per dollar. These are respected and upheld as they are bonding and are done to appease our ancestral spirits. Because she will be pregnant, some tribes in Mthwakazi may straight away call for dowry package, which, generally, is always last when the couple will have settled well with children in their marriage. In Mthwakazi culture and religion, dowry, which we call *lobolo*, is paid to the girl's parents and is not needed right away; it is also not a way of selling our daughters but a way of blending families together. Arrangements for a wedding begin after such meetings.

In the case of proposals for marriage where there is no pregnancy, the boy's family initiates and takes the first steps, although the meetings will take place at the girl's home. The boy's family sends a go-between to the girl's family; he must be good at marriage rites and a good negotiator, must be respected in community. He will be directed to a junior uncle and request the marriage between their daughter and his friend's son.

This junior uncle will have known that this emissary would come and somehow will have made consultations with his family beforehand to be able to respond without being hurtful. The junior uncle will send the emissary back with a promise to respond to the proposal in the earliest time after taking it along the correct stages or protocols. This may take time, as the girl's family is not obliged to do their act according to the boy's time speed. The girl's family will meet and assign an aunt to the issue to search the girl and indicate to her that such was on the family matters for consideration. She will, of course, be aware of this and will have given the green light for the issue to begin; rarely do we find at such a stage girls moving out of the idea and even abscond because of fear and shame of her peers. When she settles with her aunt, a meeting will then be arranged between the families. The uncle sends word through his daughter to the boy who, in turn, tells his family to alert the emissary to lead them to that meeting. The procedure then takes shape as in the case above. Some tribes in Mthwakazi bring a number of girls for the boy to identify his girl, and the rest are sent away. This is done to introduce serious business and openly that in the next or on coming, this one girl singled out of the rest, though younger than some who may be there, has stopped playing hide-and-seek as she has chosen to marry. Mthwakazi culture has token charges that may be imposed here just as a matter of convenience and respect of our culture. The *Angaziwe* may have meanings that may vary accordingly; some take it as introductive, yet some take it subjectively. The *Isivula mlom'* is a charge just to persuade us to begin discussing your issue because it is not our fault that we are here but your choice. All these charges are less than when the girl is pregnant; they are more amicably received and paid than when the girl is pregnant. These petty payments are used for the food and drinks that may be consumed soon after the discussions are over. These are exchanges of love and understanding between the two families. These help cement relationships.

When all proposals are finished, and what follows is the departure of the bride to her groom's home, a special rite is performed on her in the house and finished in the kraal. The ancestral spirits (a*madlozi*) must be told that their granddaughter is leaving the home, and the spirits must look after her where she is going. Good luck, long life, fertility, and prosperity are very important; hence, Mthwakazi religious beliefs come from our gone ones who supplicate on our behalf, and we believe these spirits reside in our kraals. The head of the family will call upon all the members of the family who have gone before us to bless the girl. He will also prepare medicine aimed at bringing prosperity to the girl while looking after her new home at her husband's family. We call the magico-medicine *Isithundu*. Today this is done after the wedding ceremony, just as the bride leaves her home for the groom's home. in our rural setup, we celebrate at the girl's home first, then the following day, we do the same at the bridegroom's home and leave the bride in her new home. The head of the family, after praying to our ancestral spirits and blessing the bride and handing her the medicine, leads her to the kraal where he will guide her around the kraal but inside then walk her out of the kraal, holding her hand. She is advised to shout away all bad spells she can remember and ask for all the blessings as guided by the head of the family. While the service is going on, a wax candle, *ibaso*, is prepared and will be burning a mixture of medicines designed to invoke the spirits to enlighten the girl's way to her new home. All these activities going on and taking place, a religious rite goes with them; special symbols for special rites are employed that indicate that man cannot live without faith and trust and hope because his future is an affair that is tied up with thought and action. His hopes for success life with his faith in the glorious power of the spirits of the invisible one. Each day he acts on reasonable probabilities, and when we take risks and stumble, Mthwakazi believes it will be the spirits that determine the outcome. We believe one day we will join the spirits in the world of the dead, but we will intercede potentially as a god for our children, and because of this faith, each one of us feels conscientiously religious and responsible. our belief in the immortality of humanity makes us prepare for the glorious life after physical death, the life of a god that has power to influence and protect the living. To Mthwakazi, god has no form he can link to but is classified as a spirit that can create. He can only be approached through the ancestral spirits (*amadlozi*); hence, we dedicate all of us into their hands and humble ourselves before our spirits from inception. We believe the ancestral spirits consult with god and seek his advice before responding to calls by the living. In the mind of the people of Mthwakazi, the sequentially in prayer seems so indelible in that we mind more to please our immediate dead to impress on them to intercede with god the creator. It is to us un-cultural to omit our father and jump to our father, the creator of heaven and earth, without our procreator, my father gideon dube. The important fact is the manifestation and invocation of the power of the ancestral spirits, which clearly encountered, and we experience in dreams, taboos, and omens that remind us when we go away from the wishes and demands of our god in heaven. The connection to us is clear and works wonders like Jews would say the god of abraham, isaac, and Jacob.

After the bride arrives at the groom's home and those that accompany her are gone, she begins new life with new relations that demand adjustments at otherwise all fronts. Instead of her parents, she has a mother-in-law and father-in-law; a lot must just fit if she has to lead a happy life. The way she respects them and humbles herself to them will determine her good stay there in her new home. Once she succeeds in winning their respect, she will enjoy being their daughter, even better than, hitherto, at her original home. Here, she carries her own dignity and her husband's together because the in-laws are aware the consequences will be high to disturb her as this will also disturb him unless otherwise. When she makes ready food, she will include her father-in-law and mother-in-law until when they decide to give her authority to move away from the main kitchen to her own and her husband and children; to some it takes a year or so. If she were the last in line of age of the boys in the home, she may take over the main kitchen and be responsible for their parents, especially if they are old.

The procreation of children is consummation of marriage between the two spouses, and the ancestral spirits when we declare (*amadlozi avumile*) the spirits have accepted. During gestation period, some clans announce the pregnancy to the ancestors early so that they protect the child at the earliest stages. The expecting mother drinks certain medicines so that the passage for the child will open and make it slippery. Mthwakazi people believe that a donkey's placenta and the skin of a python are good medicines, which, if drunk in soup during pregnancy, will make the children just come out easily. Mthwakazi women train elderly women as midwives to attend to women when they deliver. When the woman is about to deliver, she goes into the house and calls a midwife to attend to her. When delivery is through, the placenta is separated from the umbilical cord; a sharp tool is used. Some clans bury the placenta in an anthill or compost heap. Most clans, particularly the royal clan, the Khumalo, treat the placenta the same way as the umbilical cord. These are taken on a stub to a river and chipped on a rock as fish take the pieces away. This is a sign that the wife was faithful. Some clans also close to the royal clan treat the placenta alike but keep the umbilical cord until the child can walk, then they tie the cord with a cloth loosely around the neck or the waist of the child who will be carefully watched to see where the cloth drops, then it is swept and thrown into the river, or today, in urban center, it is flushed into the toilet. Some royal clans believe this is why the majority does not eat seafoods. In the early stages of giving birth, the woman and child are kept in isolation for some time, and people will come and kneel at the doorway and say congratulations (*amhlophe*), which is repeated when the placenta and the umbilical cord are treated. This expression acclaims great thanks to the spiritual snakes for having saved the infant from what Mthwakazi believes is a dreadful stage of life. We believe that two lives were living together, and now they are separated, and each can live independently thereafter. The mother is given medicine from roots and herbs to make her develop enough milk to feed the child. The man must hunt for a kill for her to get enough food; if the family is well-to-do, a slaughter is done so that she can drink a lot of salty warm soup for good health, which is important for the child too.

like in the bible, where children were initiated, the Mthwakazi people too do the same and done in two stages. The first is done as early as the time when the placenta and the umbilical cord are treated. The child is received into the community in which it is to live as a new member and must be given a name and identification. The child may be given one of his ancestors' name for a memorial or, in some cases, to invoke the spirit of the ancestor so that it may bless the household. Mthwakazi believes that the longer time expires between the dead and the living, the more we forget each other, the less the dead spirit can remain influential to the lives of the living. By giving the name to one of the born children, we believe we invoke or bring the spirit of our ancestors alive among us while others describe the life in the home. Nearly all Mthwakazi names mean something and interpret events that take place in the neighborhood at the time the child is born. If the ancestor was an *inyanga*, it does not mean the grandchild will be one as well. Intimacy for the dead and the belief that they care for the living make us think of them and desire and long to see them. Hence, if their names are called upon our children, we feel better and hopeful. Belonging to a family means living in close communication with the dead and the living. Being part of a family, therefore, means belief in the living and the dead as an entity. All this is thought of at the first initiation of the child. Remember the female child is treated the same as the male child, but she takes after her aunts or grandmothers.

The second initiation takes place at the age of ten years or so, when children of the same age in the same neighborhood are brought together for otherwise mark cutting. Depending on what marks are common within a community, some make marks on ears, some under the eyes. These marks explain what they mean and what they protect because they are not only marks but also preventive treatments. Elevens under eyes help eyesight and those holes on ears help bleeding or fluid emptive ears through today they can be used for earrings. These initiations that involve body cuts are done in winter, when the weather is cold, to avoid possible infections. These cuttings too are more human than spiritual; hence, some children may not undergo this and is not imperative of the spirit to so the initiation. it is important, however, to offer the cutting tools of instruments to the dead before service starts, which may not be necessary as these tools must have been used several times before. it is also very important to be skillful in the cutting as some may cause severe bleeding. a reed of a stick without bark is pushed through the cut so that it heals and leaves the hole. a few clans make holes through the nose, but it is restricted to a few tribes, especially those that came and now reside around the Zambezi Valley in northwest Mthwakazi. Both girls and boys are to undergo these rites, which are symbols of acceptance and entry into the society. After the service is through, the initiates line up and shake hands with parents and friends to be welcomed into Mthwakazi community as full members of the clan and tribe.

The third stage of growth is a crucial stage for both boys and girls, the adolescence, a time at which they undergo manhood and womanhood training. it is at this age that they show rudeness and arrogance. it is this time that character shapes, yet it is also during this time when new teaching makes very little change on them. Boys herd cattle in the bush, and they are shown what herbs and roots to dig and eat that help develop their muscles and harden their skin; the herbs help in the formation of sperm to aid development to full puberty. The girls begin to develop breasts; some who are fast may begin their menstruation flow. a lot of guidance and training begins at this stage, and once spoiled, they become difficult to bring back into productive citizens.

The fourth stage, puberty, occurs to both boys and girls. When a boy enters this stage, he realizes this when he has wet dreams for the first time, when he emits sperms while asleep. He is taught at adolescence that when this occurs, he must wake up early in the morning and go and bathe at the river. He must pull river grass that has corners and tie it around his waist. When he comes back from the river, he comes to sit at the fireplace at the cattle kraal (*edale*). he must be found there still naked and cold, and a fire is made for him. Some clans thrash him with twigs to strengthen his body. He is sent to herd cattle that day naked, except for the river grass around his waist. He is instructed not to sit down, except on an anthill, and will only come home at sunset. If no doctor comes to give him treatment, the routine may go on for a week, and when at last the doctor comes, herbs are put in his food, which is made hard and dry and difficult to swallow. The doctor makes him lick and sniff a food rite (*udengezi*). This is made up of burned stuff from little creatures, like scorpions, hornets, and flesh of smallclawed animals like wildcats, honey badgers, and rodents, all burned together in a potsherd called *udengezi*. These are pounded into the fire powder, which is mixed with mild, to make a paste, and then the young man licks it from the palms of his hand as he says a spell. His father welcomes him as a man and gives him a beast as a token of manhood. These are lessons on the duties of a father and what it means to be a man. The young man is taught how to settle disputes, especially in a polygamous situation; some clans joined into forces and cannot marry before they complete a stint in the impis. Some are assigned to a hunting trip, given the spear axe, bow, and arrows; and to qualify at the top of men, one must kill a lion, leopard, or any man-eater. Celebrations will follow such, and girls will be told about the young man and will be looking forward to be quoted by him. He joins from the men and leaves the boys. At puberty, the girl's first experience of menstruation sometimes makes her cry, but like the boys at adolescence, she is taught what to do when she finds herself in it. She tells her mother who prepares some porridge, red bitter corn, or sweet reed. The porridge is called *isinyayi* because it is mixed with soot from the thatch of their huts. This makes her aware and stable when such repeats. Under normal circumstances, this will happen every month once and at regular times. She may even realize when she is about to have it.

After a year, neighbors and other girls who have had the same experience are invited to a feast, and celebrations go on through the night. At dawn, the girls go to the river to bathe and come back and continue dancing and feasting until sunset. Some communities attack her while naked to stiffen her against such from her husband in the future. Lessons of how to be a good housewife begin right away, like care of children, behavior toward men, and use of sex; senior women of the village teach good cookery. It is a scorn or taboo to divorce in our culture, and infidelity was punishable by death. Today cross-cultural tendencies have weakened our religion. Regulation of sex is taught to girls after the puberty rite because these girls can now accept marriage proposals, and they can be ready to be sent away into marriage by their parents because it was otherwise the father's privilege to choose an in-law for himself, even if the man was married or was older than her.

Both the boys and the girls after these rites are considered grown-ups and can be consulted for family decisions.

CHAPTER EIGHT

RELATIONSHIP AND HOMEMAKING

Mthwakazi people and religion believe in a pluralistic family. When we talk of relatives or relationships, we mean really a broad spectrum of heads of homes and even families tied together by a single ancestor, a founder, or biblically, a patriarch, like abraham, isaac, and Jacob. Relations can be by clans; they can be by totem. Relations also occur at marriages, when two families become inlaws and create permanent relations because of the marriage. Much respect is given to men who have many wives and children. Their kraals are of enormous sizes. The more wives a man has the more he is dignified. When his sons marry, the kraal increases further in size and population. The spirit of unity must prevail in the home, if peace and tranquility have to be maintained. Respect for one another brings about harmonious relations. Prosperity is accorded to the unity of purpose among the members of the family. The ancestral spirit blesses the family when there is respect and love between the spouses. The living father takes charge and initiates the running of the home. His instructions are considered to be representatives of the spirit of the ancestors. He is the eldest man of the family and can offer the water libation to the spirits if the children are ill. The eldest wife is also the controller of the women.

The relations in the home do not only stress on blood relationship but also goes even into friendship among the family members. All the boys born of all the women in the polygamy are brothers and the girls are sisters. They can never marry because incest is punishable by death. It is considered bewitching or wizardly and can cause dire hardships in the home. Adultery is also punishable by death as it causes hatred and disrespect among the family members. Only in the case of impotence can a woman be advised to take her husband's brother to make children for him. The doctor must have failed. Otherwise, he can make the young man productive magically. The cordial relations in the home makes all men eat together and women together too. This makes it easy to realize those filled with hate or malice.

In choosing a spouse, tribalism has always been considered paramount among the Mthwakazi people because of the role played by the indwelling spirits. These can easily break a marriage bond between spouses whose language, customs, and spiritual life differ from each other. Related clans or groups of tribes have similar spirits, which will be heard when a water libation is offered. The marriage must, of course, not be exogamous, as a dube must not marry a dube or a Khumalo must not marry a Khumalo. When a woman marries, she immediately grafts into her husband's family. Today our wives like to be called by the totems of their husbands because it will be easy to identify with her children, as they will be called by the totem of their father. The disposition and personality of the man, whether he was married or not, counts a great deal in marriage and homemaking. This is because proposing love to a girl was not and do not in keeping with Mthwakazi customs because marriage is in seniors and families arrange our custom may enjoy just a matter of exchange. The spouses' parents will be friends, and it would be disturbing to mistreat each other when your parents are great friends.

The day the girl leaves for the groom's home, a special rite is performed on her in the house and then in the kraal. The spirits must be told that she is leaving the home and must look after her where she is going. Good luck and long life, fertility and prosperity, are paramount, and these can only be gotten from the sleeping men besides the kraal. The head of the kraal will call upon all the dead he can recall to bless the girl. Spells may be said as the man prepares medicine for her, measured to bring prosperity (*isithundu*). she may say some spells repeating her guide. She must be able to recall some of these spells as she may be required to say them when in temporary problems. a wax candle (*ibaso*) is mixed with different kinds of medicines designed to invoke the spirits to lighten their daughter's way to her new home. When the bride leaves the cattle kraal, she goes straight to the groom's home. She must not look back and must arrive there at sunset. A bridal team accompanies her, which will include an aunt, who today will be the matron of honor and young sisters and cousins. On the man's side, a brother will be head of the family, the spokesperson of the wedding, and will lead the reception of his sister-in-law.

Here at her new home, she really acquaints and must be fused into the life and culture her husband grew up in. She familiarizes with all that happens at this new home. She also endeavors to adapt and learn all the culture of her new people because she has come to build a home and increase her husband's clan. Her children will be called by his name, and she will feel happy to be identified by or with his people. If her husband is a king, she automatically becomes the queen of his clan. Her children become princes and princesses. Our belief is that women have no fixed nationalities; they can adapt anyhow and anywhere. Similarly in the bible, women are not counted in census for war planning.

If she becomes pregnant for the first time, at delivery, when she gets her firstborn, she must go back to her former home to be with her mother. This was done for her own parents to train her in ways of handling the delivery of children. if it is so painful that she cries loudly, this must not happen when she does it for the second child, which she now can deliver under her husband's midwives. Complications are seen more during first child, and a norm is realized, and the next children are delivered in an expected way with safety and guarantees realized hitherto. her mother teaches her how to handle the placement and her cleanliness. after a week or a fortnight, her family sends her back to her husband. an aunt accompanies her. The husband will have visited her even at hospital, if they are those who now live mixed cultures. The husband will bring necessities for both the mother and the baby. Mthwakazi believes that most clothing for the child is bought when the child is born, not before, because we believe not until the child is out of the mother's womb, witches are active even at birth. The day the trio come—that is, the aunt, the bride, and the newborn baby— the groom slaughters a goat for their relish, and the aunt will do our customary magico-medicine for the new mother to develop enough milk in her breasts for the baby to be fed well. Some clans give names to their children at this stage. Some call them by their totems until such time or at initiation. Most Mthwakazi names mean something and/or interpret some event that took place in the vicinity at the time the child was born. Some names have effects on the behavior of the child in future, although not all children given religious names will later become spirit mediums or inyanga, like their ancestors they got the names from.

Love for the dead and the wish for them to care for us and be present with us make us choose to give our children these religious names because we feel we bring them closer to us; hence, we develop comfort, hope, and belonging. Through the name of a child among us whose name was our ancestor's makes us feel we are living in close communication with the dead who we believe are always supplicating for the living, and by this, to our religion, the dead and the living are an entity, coexisting in a community.

CHAPTER NINE

DEATH AND BURIAL

Mthwakazi family is a unit, which must maintain its integrity in life today and in life to come. Mthwakazi believes death is not an accident but a necessary end of everyone born by a woman and looks forward to finding joy in communicating spiritually with their dead, a link that never breaks, now and forever. Once you are born and you begin to know your own, you live with them here on earth; at death, you will follow them and meet them again. This is a controversial subject and shall be dealt with more in detail when we study how the dead and the living keep in communication. Our difference with the christians is that the idea of hell is absent in our religion. To Mthwakazi, every person at death meets up to the requirements set by our creator. Unlike the biblical story of lazarus on abraham's chest while divers the rich tormented in the flames of hell. At the occasion of death, the corpse is placed in a death hut behind the door, and senior men in the home get busy on the corpse, closing the eyes and the mouth and giving it the correct posture for the grave. The wife of the dead man must cover herself in a blanket, weep, and lament, while the men discuss the next steps. The property of the dead man is gathered together and must not be used until after a year. Only few or relatives of the dead man may enter the death hut and sit usually in deep silence, which may be interrupted by loud screams of cries as it is normal that such is heard whenever a relative arrives for the first visit. Some mourners break down when they just arrive and when told the cause of death. Untimely deaths are more painful than long illnesses. Some call for retributions long as they raise suspicion among the family members.

At dusk, a big fire is made in front of the death hut, and men from the neighborhood come and spend nights watching for intruders who are always thought to be witches who may snatch the corpse at night. Although, occasionally, reports occur when certain parts of corpses have been discovered having missing body tissues, this is unusual. If this is realized, the head of the family is notified, and serious purges are considered that will involve the *isangoma*, who can easily identify and pick the witches. During this vigil, a lot of politics and general discussions take place. Some of the teaching on the subject of death takes shape. Early in the morning, there is a search for the grave site by the head of the family, and usually, it must be among the braves of those that are already sleeping. Women sometimes indicate where they choose to be buried before they die. Men are to be buried at the cattle kraal unless, for a specific reason, he might tell his wife to advise the head of the family. If the dead man had grown sons, he could indicate to one, especially the elder son, where he chooses to be buried. Fathers, as a way of training their sons because much will be taking place whenever the father meets his sons, do this. It is a way of handing over customary responsibilities by the father to their sons. Cases have been known where the dead man has denied grave sites and a change was taken. One would ask how a dead man would refuse a grave site, yet our religion invested in taboos, omens, and general customs we believe we are shown by rocks or water, even difficulties in the digging, then we assume that the site is a wrong one. our religion too chides the idea of digging one's grave before you pass away; hence, earlier on, at child birth, we pointed out that we do not buy dresses and items for a baby not yet born. Mthwakazi believes humanity cannot stampede god; we wait until the die is cast.

While the grave is being dug, a few men will be at the side or in the kraal, skinning an ox slaughtered to accompany the dead man. We call this meat *mgovu*, and when roasted and eaten, it is eaten without salt. The ox is important in that we believe the dead need provision where they will be in the graves, awaiting their last dash to where god wants them. The second reason in our early civilization is the skin of the beast was used to wrap the corpse before it is laid in the grave. This meat is not allowed into the home. After the burial, it is roasted and eaten outside the home. The remains are hung on trees and will be eaten by those late mourners as they come. Bones are burned, mixed with herbs, and thrown into the river or pool. We avoid salt because we believe spirits do not like salt. Women help at the burial by collecting stones that will be laid upon the grave. The stones, even before they are laid upon the heap of soil, are called *intaba*, which means mountain. Some clans collect the stones before the grave is dug or during the time when the men dig the grave. Some go around when the heap of soil is about to fill the grave. This can be done by either men or married women. During the service, only men lay the stones on the grave. The custom is the stones, as brought from anywhere around, are placed on the ground separately; not one must be put upon another. it is here where Mthwakazi believes no stone shall be found upon another in the last days. only the men then put the stones on the heap of soil on the grave. They stand in a line between the scattered stones and the grave and pass one stone at a time forward to one who will be placing the stones on the grave to cover the whole surface of the grave. Respectively and in a solemn manner, the stones are passed forward, using both hands. In areas where there are no stones, tree branches are used. A type or kind of tree, *umphafa*, found in otherwise all-dry plain area of Mthwakazi is commonly used. In those areas, when only pebbles are found, these are removed from the ground together with the grass underneath and carried to the grave with both hands one at a time respectively.

When all preparations are over, a new doorway at the back of the death hut is made, and the corpse leaves the hut through it to the grave. At the grave, his firstborn son is made to stand at the head of the grave, holding his father's spear, piercing the ground. Taking the corpse through the new back doorway is a sign Mthwakazi believes that his departure is temporary; he will come back through the front door when he will be a spirit to come and live and guard or guide his family forever. The first wife's tuft of hair, *icholo*, on the back of her head is removed and thrown into the grave. This tuft is the one that indicates a woman's marital status. Mthwakazi believes that when men die, they must take their wives with them and go live as usual in spiritual unity. We believe in immortality or life after death. As the corpse is placed into the grave in sitting position or at their back facing the kraal, his heir stands by the grave, holding a spear, indicating that he takes over the headship of the family symbolized in the father's spear, which he now holds and possesses. The wives sit close to the grave with their faces covered. This takes place in dead silence, except for one during the internment or the service. The interment is we believe the offering of the soul of the dead to the community of the dead. The roman catholic church in Mthwakazi now leads this important part of the service, where we call upon our forebears to receive their son as they allowed that he departs from the land of the living.

Treatment of the grave is done not very differently as some clans do it before the corpse is lowered into the grave; some do it after. This rite can be twofold to protect the corpse from witches digging the grave and pulling out the dead. As Mthwakazi believes they feed on the flesh of the dead, it is also a treatment to induce unity between the dead and the living in spirits. Some common practice is to put pegs around the corpse inside the grave and assist the communion and deification of the dead father. When relatives throw handfuls of soil into the grave, they pronounce farewell, "go in peace and plead for us where you are going." During the interment service, names of all the dead fathers are mentioned, and each is asked to receive and keep the dead man an actual committal of the soul. Many believe the spitting of saliva on the soil to be thrown into the grave is symbolic, sending him victoriously and praising names of the dead and an inducement for accommodation yonder. at the end of the internment, men gently lay service the corpse, if covered with soil and the stones on the ground. The area around the grave is cleaned so that the relatives are able to detect if witches have tampered with the place at night. When the work is over, people are given a herb to wash in the river or pool. Today the *intelezi* is put in a dish at the entrance into the home from the graveyard, and people wash before they come into the home. Only our hands are washed to spell away the bad luck that we believe goes with handling a funeral. The Jews considered one unclean for at least seven days when you were in contact with a dead body. They underwent a cleansing ceremony to be accepted to do the normal duties in the community. Mthwakazi religion has a belief similar to the Jews. Close relatives gather outside the home to be treated by an *inyanga* or a herbalist who will approach them with a concoction called *umaluleka* or *umhabulo*, which is intended to purify the family of the bereaved. This rite, a mixture of a variety of herbs, roots, and leaves, is thrown onto the faces and bodies of the members of the dead person's family. They are also required to sip some of the water spit and swallow a bit of this, rinsing their mouths. As they do this, the herbalist guides them in dictated words that send away fear and wish the family to be protected from other such mishappenings in the near future. The rite is connected to the ancestral spirits who must look after and protect the ones left behind by the death of their member.

A few women smear the death hut with cow dung mixed with herbs and is done while the men are still burying the corpse. This is done to spell away the smell and drive the infection away and the magic powers that might have caused the death. Mthwakazi believes that fear of death and suffering come first in the people after the burial is done when the bereaved really comes to grips with the reality of the loss. The treatment, therefore, is very important both physically and psychologically. Mthwakazi believes this magicocleansing pushes death away for a while and gives the bereaved trust and hope. a day after the burial, a rite called *inkubalo* is performed. A goat is slaughtered, and its meat is mixed with herbs, and a protective spell is sung over this. Milk can also be used in place of meat. The herbs are mixed with milk, and the mixture is sipped during the treatment by the *inyanga*. The goat meat is roasted, and people bite apiece, while the herbalist is knocking their limb joints one at a time. This rite is more than just strengthening the family. It is also a way of immunizing them against possible mystical or highly religious mishappenings as it expresses the fundamental reliance on the spiritual powers of the ancestral spirits. Mishandling these may cause more problems. One must be careful not to open a Pandora's box. Mthwakazi religion believes that there are some spirits that must be avoided at any cost, or they are called for special occasions only a week after the burial; all the tools that were used at the burial are to be cleaned and picked by their owners. Our religion believes the owners brought these tools at the time of the digging of the grave and burial of the dead person. We do not go out to borrow pick and shovels, but everyone finds it a duty to bring a tool. A rite is performed on this day. We call this rite *izikhuba* or *ingcekeza*, which means dirt; hence, we meet to clean our tools of this dirt. Beer accompanies this ceremony of washing implements. An *inyanga* is engaged to come and conduct the rite. He will treat the beer first with *umuthi* so that contamination is removed from the tools. He sprays the tools with this beer, and people who come to collect their tools also drink the beer, this time just as a food. In this rite, no spirits are called, as it is mere ablution of the implements. After the tools are sprayed with beer, they are placed where the owners can see them and collect them. Again, these are brought as usual because when a death occurs, mostly men bring any tool they can get hold of for the purpose of digging the grave; they do not wait for the bereaved to ask for these tools. At this ceremony, many prefer the idea of getting a drink and a chat because it is after seven days, a period of getting the feel of the reality of their neighbor really gone, and here, they talk about it freely.

Our religion in Mthwakazi believes that the dead are to be called back home where they will come and dwell with us in spirit. after a year or more, a date is set for the calling or bringing back home of the dead father. The rite is called *umbuyiso* and is usually done in spring before the rains begin to fall. The safest months in Mthwakazi are september and october. Remember, Mthwakazi is in the southern hemisphere, within the tropics. The elders of the family gather to deal with the preparations for the service. Corn is soaked in water by the oldest member of the family and pronounces to the dead by name. "This is your beer. We are bringing you home so that you can look after your family and children." on the day the beer is to be squeezed, one calabash is set aside for the spirits to drink at night. The service begins at sunset at the grave. a goat is brought to the grave to offer to the dead person. This is done to appease the person and induce the dead person to come home. The goat is driven back into the home and is slaughtered to the spirits. a branch can be dragged from the grave into the home, while others sip beer and talk or say a wish then pour some beer onto the grave and walk toward home, singing a song that calls him home. "*Woza ekhaya*" is sung repeatedly by the group walking toward home. The goat is roasted and consumed the same night. During the feasting on the goat, a lot of snuff is sniffed at regular intervals. At this service, every member of the family may ask for whatever from the ancestral spirits. What remains of the goat and a calabash of beer together with snuff are placed in the hut over night for the spirits to feast and drink too. An ox would have been slaughtered in the day and left for the night in the hut. In the morning, before sunrise or dead at sunrise, there is singing and dancing as men pull the grass away from the dead man's hut. Beer is poured to the ground as libation when people dance and sing a ballad "*ubaba makeze ekhaya*," father should come home. The ox meat is roasted, and beer is served. The beer left in the night for offering will be given to the relatives when all other people are gone. Among the relatives, one of them, especially a young boy, is made to stand and pretend to be the dead man, more so if the man was a spirit medium. The young boy may be called by the dead man's name from henceforth. This communion sacrifice can be summed in this belief that the readmission of the dead man into the home in another form rather than a normal birth shows the belief by the people of Mthwakazi in the reality of immortality and, hence, the need to appease the spirits of the dead. None dies and disconnects with his folk in the land of the living. This sharing of the sacrificial meal secures a permanent acceptance and ever-lasting communication between the living and the dead. Nevertheless, the relationship is not exactly the same as that of god and man or creator and creature. The purpose of the sacrifice is to express or establish a relation of harmony and unbroken fellowship between the dead and the living. When the spirits eat and drink the food given them, they, in turn, will provide security and prosperity to the living. Because the relationship or connection between the living and the dead is vital for both, the living and the dead, this event is done annually as celebrations and commemorations.

When the dead man has come home, for leaders and royalty, we believe, once or so in the year, the living may see in the village an unusual animal, such as a leopard with three legs, or the ordinary man may appear as a snake of queer features. When we see these in our homes or in our hedges, we feel visited. Mthwakazi believes the dead turn into such creatures if they are to be seen physically. We call these *amadlozi*, and when these creatures are seen around our homes, we do not kill them. Mthwakazi believes that a dead person's spinal cord undergoes some metamorphosis, resulting in the formation or in the birth of these creatures, which represent our *amadlozi*. These, we believe, are good and most helpful to the nation as a whole and to us because they are the soul of the nation and our religion. Our religion believes that we can live in close contact with our spirits by placing them on special hosts in the home. The head of the family or even the king is placed on a black bull. This animal is installed on the day of *umbuyiso* as the host animal, *inkomo yamadlozi*. You need to know that our religion's externalism reflects its internalism and gives both ritual and human values. It is a spirit-centered religion with intellectual acceptance of an infallible system that of the supernatural powers of the dead. The ox now in the kraal represents the dead old man. Mthwakazi believes the man has come back home and will look after the family just as he did hitherto. The difference is that this time he does it through omens and dreams or such signs. When there is a catastrophe in the home or community, the senior citizens consult across the relevant levels, and prayers are brought to these spirit hosts. Our religion believes these are told in harsh terms that if they sleep and let the nation starve or the nation destroyed or defeated at war, then they have become a shame too. When there is an illness in the home, we believe the spirits will have let loose their defense; hence, these prayers are aimed at reawakening them or reminding them of their responsibility. As a nation, Mthwakazi compares herself with other nations, and the better we do or fare in any sphere of life, the more we adore our spirits. The defeat of our spirits by other spirits in interceding with our creator is our defeat too. If the spirits cannot protect their living ones, then they have absconded their duties. This vehement talk is given to the bull in the kraal, and usually, the bull rises and urinates as a sign that the spirits have heard the prayer and do appreciate the responsibility given to them. a water libation through the mouth is used, *ukumumatha*; some call it *ukukhafula*; and an annual food, drink, and snuff offering is done to appease and keep the connection between the dead and the living. All the members of the family expect some blessings from the spirits of the ancestors at least once every year. We refer to our ancestors as *abadala*, the old, or *izinyoka*, the snakes. Mthwakazi believes that the fertility of the land, the livestock, the health of the nation are all attributed to the cooperation and direction given by the spirits of our ancestors. As such, all what our nation is, Mthwakazi believes, is directed and controlled by our ancestral spirits. According to Mthwakazi religion, the dead and the living support each other in a very dependable manner. Respect for each other is, therefore, of paramount importance. It is easy for the living to realize that the spirits are not happy and must do something to appease them. What the living must have is faith in their gone ones, that the spirits will never abandon them. A lot of faith, therefore, determines the believers' ability to hold on without doubt. Great is the love, pride, and adoration between the spirits of the dead and the living.

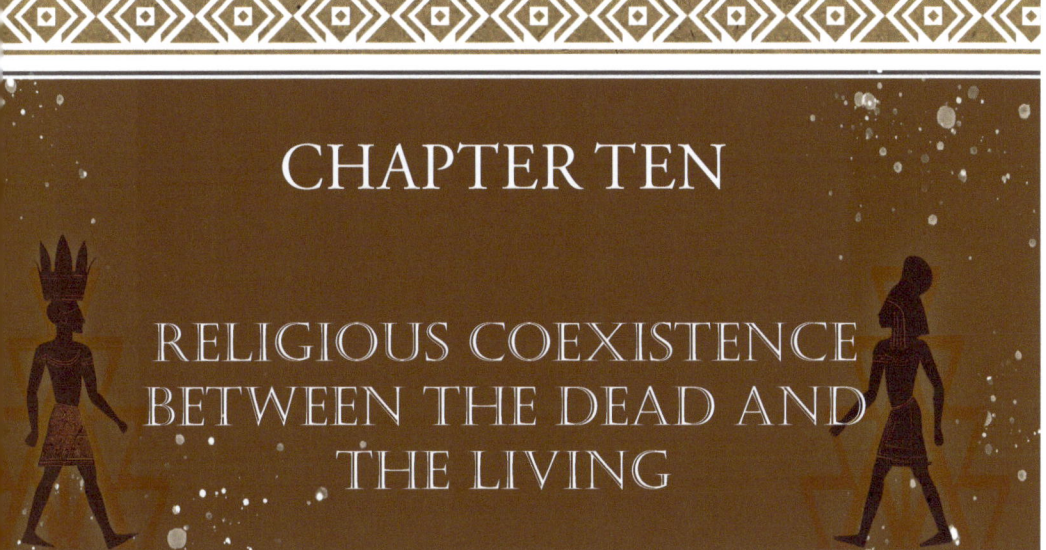

CHAPTER TEN

RELIGIOUS COEXISTENCE BETWEEN THE DEAD AND THE LIVING

The religion of Mthwakazi believes in dreams. Like the Jewish believers, dreams matter a lot to us as a nation and as a religion. Dreams, to us, are revelations and warnings directly from our ancestors. Mthwakazi believes in the close connection of our dead ones, and our creator consider dreams with high regards. Dreams make the dead and the living coexist and interact very well. Dreams maintain the almost tangible connection between the living and the dead. There are good and bad dreams. one can understand what the dream means through many such dreams, or there be a dream interpreter among you, like Joseph in egypt during the Pharaoh dynasty. Mthwakazi believes that among us, there are people who are thus gifted by providence to be able to dream or interpret dreams and connect the spirits of the dead to the lives of the living. These people are like prophets in our midst who will receive our creator's word to discriminate to us the command from our spirits that are gone. Such people were found in the age of the bible, when we read of seers who could be consulted on almost everything, including just small things like a missing flock of sheep. Mthwakazi believes that such people among us are placed to be able to connect the nation to its creator. Occasionally, when such leaders wanted to wage a war against its enemies, such dreamers would forecast the possible outcome. Mthwakazi went on war after consultations with such seers. We believe if the seer acknowledges and accepts the idea, then it must be god's wish that the task be tackled. The seer consults intensely with the spirit of the gone ones, amadlozi, who, we believe, will reveal to the seer without hesitation what to deliver to the nation.

For my teaching purpose, we will choose many of the common dreams, which serve as warnings and appraisals among Mthwakazi people, which do not need or demand for a seer to interpret. There could be differences among clans of the nation on what meanings can be drawn from what the clan has chosen as common after following the interpretation of a dream until it becomes an acceptable revelation once you dream that similar dream. A few common ones for a sick person to dream when he is well may denote death. This occurs many times that it even affects our mind-sets that when you fall ill, you will hate to dream when you are well. In the modern world, you would feel encouraged when you dream that you are well because we believe dreams produce just the opposite of what you dream. Our seers will tell you that you will lose a race or game if you dream winning it. As such, for a sick person, to dream dying, they will tell you that you will live to recover and be well again. If the following morning you wake up and sneeze then tell your death dream, then they will straightaway tell you that you will be well soon. You feel encouraged and even try to do things on your own, even though you had succumbed hitherto. if you dream seeing farm products, you will be told that it foretells riches or immediate gains in way of money. There are specific farm products that may have a specific meaning, like red corn, we call it rapoko, commonly used for brewing beer. When you dream of this repeatedly, it will instruct what you have to do with the corn. In general, when you dream of any fields and greens, then you are counted as blessed and your ways, your health, and your general life in good perspective. Dreaming of water, as long as it is clear, you are considered blessed too. Rivers, the waters therein clear and clean, are a blessing too, especially when you cross them. if they are roaring, then this denotes hardships. To dream seeing sea animals, especially fish, swimming in shallow clear water, then you can always be encouraged. Success is foretold when you dream running water, but stagnant dirty water warns you possible problems soonest. Dreaming of climbing or sitting on heights then denotes success or promotion at work. All green vegetation denotes good health and happiness. If dream anything taken away from you, even cutting of your hair, then you must expect some loss in any way. If your hair is removed, then there would be a death of a relative.

Whereas dreaming bad things may mean good things, it is not good to dream of witches because this tells you of their presence in the house. Mthwakazi fears witches, and we believe they are angels of the devil. When you dream about them, you even feel your breath running out as if they were sitting on your chest. After such a dream, inyanga may cast the spell away and reassert you home defenders as we believe a home is protected by magic that is dug at the four corners of one's home. For the witches to be in the house and you dream of them, then something must be wrong. Light rain or showers are good as this denotes prosperity. To see a pit and that you fall into it is bad as it means a funeral of a close relative or even you, the dreamer. Mthwakazi believes the one who dreamed when birds ate up what he was carrying was tried and beheaded, as in the bible. So you can dream of your fate. Dreaming of animals, cattle, are good when they look fat; donkeys are bad, although, biblically, christ chose to ride on a colt. If you dream of a veld fire, it denotes that you will be in trouble and that your enemies will overcome you. If you dream your home is on fire, it denotes serious troubles and misery. If you dream eating honey, it is good, but when bees sting you, it is bad and denotes gossip about you by your friends or associates. For young people to dream flying denotes success in their lives. If you dream you are drowning, it is not good because it indicates loss, even in a lawsuit or demotion, if you hold a position at work. For a young man or woman to dream of snakes denotes pregnancy. For a young man to dream losing a tooth denotes that his girlfriend's love is fading. To dream weeping foretells happiness and merriment. The eclipse of the sun or moon is bad; it shows decline in all positive rewards. Many people's dreams mean the opposite of what they dream, but in each community or home, a few dreams exactly what the dream means, and these are the custodians of the connection between the living and the dead. Mthwakazi calls such people panic-mongers. Such are sometimes treated by a herbalist to defer such dreadful dreams because Mthwakazi does not enjoy knowing disasters before they occur because we believe god's way cannot be deranged by humans. The panic-monger is required to wear the muthi around his neck or place it under the pillow to stop him from dreaming big at night. Dreams reveal or make us know how strong the link is between the dreamer and our ancestors, and Mthwakazi believes we are visited in our sleep by these spirits. Mthwakazi people believe ancestral spirits visit us in our sleep and talk to us in dreams. If you were deciding to buy a tractor made in china and you dream seeing your money in a pit, you will definitely change your minds and refrain from buying the tractor.

Careful study of dreams is necessary if they are to be used as guiding instincts among us. To those that are not panic-mongers, if you go to bed with a heavy stomach after eating heavily, you will have numerous dreams that you will hardly remember, and most of them will be just nightmares. Mthwakazi believes they are not all dreams that matter; also, not all dreamers are representative of the connection between the nations and the ancestral spirits, hence the need for a thorough study of the dreams and the dreamer. If you go to bed thirsty, you may dream seeing water and drinking it; some of the dreams are recollections of what you did or experienced in the day. This may just be the subconscious at work; you may be heard talking or even singing the actions that you were doing in the day. Mthwakazi calls this *ukuwumana* and has nothing to do with our ancestral spirits. The central belief on dreams in Mthwakazi is that our long dead speak to the living through dreams. We also believe the creator talks to us through dreams. Our day-to-day interactions are guided and controlled through dreams. if you committed a serious crime like the King of egypt and had taken sara, abraham's wife, he was warned through a dream not to touch her. Even today we respect dreams, and we believe even some of the greatest achievements in history were revealed to nations through dreams. We, therefore, believe dreams connect us too well and continuously to our spirits and our god and creator. We believe, if god spoke, his voice would be too frightening for us to listen and hear, for it will be like thunder; hence, in our sleep, we can get the messages. How do we keep this in memory until daybreak is the question that is part of our teaching among our people. When you dream and you wake up soon after the dreams are over, you are required to turn your pillow over, and this will make you remember your dream in the morning. We also believe if the message is for instructions, the spirits will make you remember the dream very well in the morning. Many play dreams are never remembered.

CHAPTER ELEVEN

SUMMARY

For a time, the religion, manner, and customs of the people of Mthwakazi had been put aside in pursuit of the god of the missionary world. When the missionary came in the seventeenth century, all our religious matters and arts were regarded as heathen and un-christian. Only through study of prehistoric religions have we come to realize that every ethnic group knew and knows god in their own way that demands respect. Hence, when Paul found in athens a statue to the unknown god, he was impressed and taught them successfully that this unknown god could really be known as he is the originator and creator of the universe, the omnipresent, omniscient, and omnipotent. Each nationality has its way known to this god as to how to interact with him. He put down ways until the coming of his son, the Messiah, then all nations shall bow and praise god through him, as he is the way, the life, and the light.

Mthwakazi people, in their religion, know the difference between god, the creator, *uMlimu, uMdali, uNkulunkulu* and our ancestral spirit *amadlozi*. *Umdali* is the first man, the creator of *uhlanga*, who is the father of the tribe. We call this idea *umdabuko*, the beginning, like the creation of adam and eve. a tribe is the offspring of the acknowledged one god. adam knew only one god, his maker, and his children could not have known any other god and creator. In the history of israel, their forefathers abraham, isaac, and Jacob are called patriarchs and are held with respect. In Mthwakazi, those that came before us and bore us are *amadlozi*, the ancestral spirits, which we believe cannot be ignored if we need success and good life that comes from god, the creator. We believe the spirit of the dead mother or father mediates for the living. a snake, *inyoka*, symbolizes *idlozi*. This protects and gives life from inception to health, wealth, and long life in the family. *Amadlozi* are of two kinds: the recent dead known to us and the spirits who are only known by their names. When one prays to *idlozi*, the recent dead accepts the prayer and passes it on to the long dead, unknown to the living except by name. The remote *idlozi*, the unknown spirits, will take the petition to *uMdali*, the creator of heaven and earth. by the same procedure, god will answer our requests. The speaker, nonetheless, does not stop at the names of the recent known dead but goes on to mention even god by according him the accepted form Mthwakazi has for god, the creator, putting him at the top of all spirits. Stating that even you who is in the clouds, *lawe osemafini*. It must suffice for my reader that the ancestral spirits are go-betweens to god and the living, although stress is on the immortality of humanity and their potential to become gods after death. In Mthwakazi religion, a religious rite accompanies all the activities in our day-to-day life. You must also realize that special symbols are attached to special religious rites. Mthwakazi believes all life is an act of adoration and worship because we believe man cannot live without faith, because his relationship with the future is an affair that ties up with thought and action. Mthwakazi's high hopes for achievement lie with his faith in the power of the invisible spirits. Each day we must act on reasonable possibilities, take risks, and concede and expect defeat as being the will of the spirit. Our potential to be gods or like our ancestors after our death makes us live more religiously today, and tomorrow will look after itself.

Our belief in the immortality of human beings makes us try to prepare for the glorious life after death. This life will be that of a spirit with power to influence the living and, though unseen, remain active in the affairs of our nation. To Mthwakazi as god has no form we can only link to when we are spirits dead but crawling spirits between our living and our uMdali the god of the universe. Mthwakazi believes that the ancestral spirits consult god and seek his advice before responding to calls by the living. The order in which Mthwakazi people pray according to our religion seems to be indelible in our minds that the christian approach least impress even the devout christians today in my nation. To live without the thought of my dead ones seems to contradict even the idea of having abraham, isaac, and Jacob as the patriarchs to israel. To the nominal christian, in my religion, it sounds uncultured and ill-mannered to leave out your cocreator with god when you pray. The manifestation and invocation of the power of the ancestral spirits, which is clearly encountered and experienced in dreams, is very important. Defiance of taboos and warnings in omens result in defective observance. In modern churches, you will find those that are still in the maze. Yet those who read the bible will realize that god put these among his creation, and they all culminate to the coming of the Messiah, when there will be no Jew, greek, or gentile, neither slave nor master. if my people in the religion and manners and customs will read and understand their religion more, how good the taboos, omens, and customs were, they will realize how god drew a way how they would be led to salvation. if my forefather became a christian yet embrace his customs and manners and he dies having been a model that was seen by my father or mother who will also live a good life as a model for me and I do the same for my children, eventually, we will realize how god used different cultures, ways, manners, taboos, and omens for the same objective that we may glorify his name from the nations we belong. Generation upon generation of those that uphold their way of worship as demanded by Jesus the way of life and the light.

There is no contradiction in the ways god has given us to know him. My ancestral spirits nurtured in god's way will speak for their living in god's way, and only the name of god shall be known all over throughout the whole world. Mthwakazi's religion, manners, omens, and taboos uphold this god of adam and eve in Jesus's name. Amen.

FOOTNOTES

David s. Noss and John b. Noss, Man's Religions: The BaVhenda of Southern Africa, 1949, p. 25.

Rev. Wallace Bozongwana, Ndebele Religions and Customs, Mambo Press, rhodesia literature bureau, 1983.

Philip Yancey, Reaching the Invisible God Beyond Our Control, 2000, p. 73. Norman Geisler, Come Let US Reason, 2001, p. 66.

David Schwartz, The Magic of Thinking Big, 1984, p. 44.

Milfred Minatrea, Shaped by God's Heart, 2004, p. 26. William grady, Final Authority God as a Spirit, 2005, p. 87.

Robert McGee, 2005, p. 87.

Robert McGee, The Search for Significance, 1998, p. 13.

Robertson McQuilkin, Understanding and Applying the Bible, 1983, p. 91. David Otis Fuller, Which Bible? 1972, p. 30.

Stayt Hugh, A Case Study of the BaVenda of Southern Africa, 1928, p. 25.

BIBLIOGRAPHY

Bozongwana, Wallace rev. Ndebele Religion and Customs. Mambo Press, The rhodesia literature bureau, 1983.

Brooks, Ronald. Come Let Us Reason Logical Thinking. Baker book house, grand rapids, Michigan, 2001.

Evans, William. The Great Doctrines of the Bible-Doctrine of the Spirit. Moody Press, Chicago, 1974.

Grady, William. Final Authority God as a Spirit-My Helpmeet. Grady Publications, Tennessee, 2005.

Hugh, Stayt. Religion in Prehistoric and Primal Cultures: The BaVenda of Southern Africa. Oxford university Press, 1928.

McGee, Robert. The Search for Significance. Word Publishing, Nashville, 1998.

McQuilkin, Robertson. Understanding the Bible and its Application. Moody Press, Chicago, 1983. 85

Minatrea, Milfred. Shaped by God's Heart. Jossey-bass a. Wiley imprint, 2004.

Schwartz, David. The Magic of Thinking Big. Simon and Schuster, London, 1984.

Yancey, Philip. Reaching the Invisible God. Zondervan, grand rapids, Michigan, 2000. 86.

www.ingramcontent.com/pod-product-compliance
Lightning Source LLC
Chambersburg PA
CBHW040934030426
42337CB00001B/7